The UN Secretary-General and Secretariat

D1607500

This book offers a keen insight into the pulsing heart of the United Nations – the Secretariat and its head, the Secretary-General – and examines what this organ does and why.

Behind the public face of the Secretary-General, Kofi Annan, and his predecessors, an active corps of officials and advisers have unceasingly applied the decisions of the "debating UN." They constitute the "acting UN" and face ceaseless pressures and challenges. They initiate or contribute to policies and activities that affect the 191 governments represented in the "debating UN." As chief officers of the UN Secretariat, the Secretaries-General have included such innovating figures as Annan and Dag Hammarskjöld.

This book sums up the history, structure and continuing operations of an ever-present global institution. The text:

- gives special attention to policy development by the Secretary-General;
- makes clear the strengths and weaknesses of the organization;
- details the solid and substantive work of the UN's permanent staff.

Written by a recognized authority on the subject, this is the ideal interpretative introduction for students of the UN, international organizations and global governance.

Leon Gordenker is Emeritus Professor of Politics and research fellow of the Princeton Institute for International and Regional Studies at Princeton University, USA. He is a long-time observer of international organization and has written extensively on the United Nations and organized transnational relationships.

Global Institutions Series

Edited by Thomas G. Weiss
The CUNY Graduate Center, New York, USA
and Rorden Wilkinson
University of Manchester, UK

The "Global Institutions Series" is designed to provide readers with comprehensive, accessible, and informative guides to the history, structure, and activities of key international organizations. Every volume stands on its own as a thorough and insightful treatment of a particular topic, but the series as a whole contributes to a coherent and complementary portrait of the phenomenon of global institutions at the dawn of the millennium.

Each book is written by a recognized expert in the field, conforms to a similar structure, and covers a range of themes and debates common to the series. These areas of shared concern include the general purpose and rationale for organizations, developments over time, membership, structure, decision-making procedures, and key functions. Moreover, the current debates are placed in a historical perspective alongside informed analysis and critique. Each book also contains an annotated bibliography and guide to electronic information as well as any annexes appropriate to the subject matter at hand.

The volumes currently under contract include:

The United Nations and Human Rights (2005)
by Julie Mertus (American University)

UN Global Conferences (2005)
by Michael Schechter (Michigan State University)

The UN Secretary-General and Secretariat (2005)
by Leon Gordenker (Princeton University)

The UN General Assembly (2005)
by M. J. Peterson (University of Massachusetts, Amherst)

The UN Security Council
by Edward C. Luck (Columbia University)

The International Monetary Fund
by James Vreeland (Yale University)

For further information regarding the series, please contact:

Craig Fowlie, Publisher, Politics & International Studies
Taylor & Francis
2 Park Square, Milton Park, Abingdon
Oxford OX14 4RN, UK

+44 (0)207 842 2057 Tel
+44 (0)207 842 2302 Fax

Craig.Fowlie@tandf.co.uk
www.routledge.com

The UN Secretary-General and Secretariat

Leon Gordenker

Routledge
Taylor & Francis Group

LONDON AND NEW YORK

First published 2005 by
Routledge
2 Park Square, Milton Park, Abingdon, Oxon OX14 4RN

Simultaneously published in the USA and Canada
by Taylor & Francis Inc
270 Madison Ave., New York, NY 10016

Routledge is an imprint of the Taylor & Francis Group

Typeset in Times and Helvetica by
Taylor & Francis Books
Printed and bound in Great Britain by
MPG Books Ltd, Bodmin

British Library Cataloguing in Publication Data
A catalogue record for this book is available from the British Library

Library of Congress Cataloging in Publication Data
A catalog record for this title has been requested

ISBN 0–415–34378–X (hbk)

Contents

Boxes

Abbreviations

ACABQ	Advisory Committee on Administrative and Budgetary Questions
ACC	Administrative Committee on Coordination
CEB	Chief Executives Board for Coordination
CHR	Commission on Human Rights
DPI	Department of Public Information
ECLAC	Economic Commission for Latin America and the Caribbean
ECOSOC	Economic and Social Council
EU	European Union
FAO	Food and Agriculture Organization
HRC	Human Rights Commission
ICAO	International Civil Aviation Organization
ILO	International Labor Organization
IMF	International Monetary Fund
NAM	non-aligned movement
NATO	North Atlantic Treaty Organization
NGOs	non-governmental organizations
NIEO	New International Economic Order
OECD	Organisation for Economic Co-operation and Development
OIOS	(UN) Office of International Oversight Services
OPEC	Organization of Petroleum-Exporting Countries
UNCHR	UN Commissioner for Human Rights
UNCTAD	UN Conference on Trade and Development
UNDP	UN Development Programme
UNEF	UN Emergency Force
UNEP	UN Environment Programme
UNESCO	UN Educational, Scientific and Cultural Organization
UNFPA	UN Population Fund

UNHCHR	UN High Commissioner for Human Rights
UNHCR	UN High Commissioner for Refugees
UNICEF	United Nations Children's Fund
WB	World Bank
WFP	World Food Programme
WHO	World Health Organization

Foreword

This volume is among the first in a new and dynamic series on "global institutions." As the title suggests, we hope that it offers a comprehensive guide to the history, structure, and concrete activities of "UN Secretary-General and Secretariat." Remarkable as it may seem, there exist few individual works that offer in-depth treatments of prominent global bodies and processes, much less an entire series of concise and complementary volumes. Those that do exist are either out of date, inaccessible to the non-specialist reader, or seek to develop a specialized understanding of particular aspects of an institution or a process rather than offer an overall account of its functioning. Similarly, existing works have often been written in highly technical language or have been crafted "in-house" and are notoriously self-serving and narrow in focus.

The advent of electronic media has helped by making information and resolutions more widely available, but it has also complicated matters further. The growing reliance on the Internet and other electronic methods of finding information about key international organizations and processes has served, ironically, to limit the educational materials to which most readers have ready access – namely, books. Public relations documents, raw data, and loosely refereed web sites do not intelligent analysis make. Official publications compete with a vast amount of electronically available information, much of which is suspect because of its ideological or self-promoting slant. Paradoxically, the growing range of purportedly independent websites offering analyses of the activities of particular organizations have emerged, but one inadvertent consequence has been to frustrate access to basic, authoritative, critical, and well-researched texts. The market for such has actually been reduced by the ready availability of varying quality electronic materials.

We are delighted that Routledge asked us to edit a series that bucks this trend. They are betting that serious students and professionals will want serious analyses. We have assembled a first-rate line-up of authors. Our intention, then, is to provide one-stop shopping for all readers – students (both undergraduate and postgraduate), interested negotiators, diplomats, practitioners from the non-governmental and intergovernmental communities, and interested parties alike – seeking information about most prominent institutional aspects of global governance.

The UN Secretary-General and Secretariat

We asked Leon Gordenker – professor emeritus at Princeton University – to undertake the daunting task of making sense of the globe's top international civil servant and the people who work for him. We could not have found a commentator with more experience or wisdom. Having begun work for the world organization as a journalist in the late 1940s and covering the Korean conflict before doing his PhD at Columbia, one of his first and most widely cited books was on the Secretary-General.[1] And much of his distinguished career as a teacher and researcher has focused on the behavior and misbehavior of international secretariats.

Lee Gordenker's concise and elegant volume will permit readers to understand the strengths and weaknesses of the international civil service and the leadership at the United Nations, which the first Secretary-General, Trygve Lie, called "the most impossible job in the world."[2] Frustrations and exasperation, yes, but also the seven occupants and their senior and junior staffs have made a difference to the rhetoric and reality of multilateral cooperation.

During the Second World War, the Carnegie Endowment for International Peace sponsored a series of conferences to learn the lessons from what many believed was the "great experiment" of the League of Nations, namely, creating a core of independent officials to attack international problems.[3] This legacy was carried over to the UN, and Charter Article 101.3 called for the "paramount consideration in the employment of staff" to be "securing the highest standards of efficiency, competence, and integrity" while paying regard "to the importance of recruiting the staff on as wide a geographical basis as possible." This book portrays the pluses and minuses of the heart and soul of the "second United Nations" – not the arena where states make decisions, but the international civil service. Our hope is that Lee Gordenker's analysis reaches a broad audience with its many useful descriptions, lists of resources, and numerous concrete examples that illustrate how people matter.

As always, we welcome comments and suggestions from readers.

Thomas G. Weiss, The CUNY Graduate Center, New York, USA
Rorden Wilkinson, University of Manchester, UK

December 2004

Preface

This book uses some of the work and experience of countless journalists, scholars, civil servants and politicians who have sought to understand the development of international organization since World War I. It is a formidable body of writing that covers a novel and growingly complex civic experience related to bringing some useful logic to the relations among all governments on earth. With gratitude, I refer in the text to this writing.

As my contact with the United Nations began in 1945, my interpretations of what the office of Secretary-General of the United Nations and the Secretariat represent are colored by early and later occasional participation and by long observation. That has helped turn this book, whether for good or ill, rather more towards the form of an essay than the systematic academic scholarship represented by much work cited below. I hope that it will help increase understanding of and curiosity about how an international secretariat functions and why its activities have their particular flavor.

In the course of thinking and writing this work, I have had the benefit of conversations – not structured interviews – with old colleagues and active and recent members of the Secretariat of low and high rank. If they recognize their contributions here, I hasten to assure them that misinterpretations, as others here, are mine. I undertook not to quote or refer specifically to these conversations in order to collect untrammeled opinions and facts and to subject my tentative conclusions to expert scrutiny.

Helpful comment also came from academic colleagues. I am grateful for criticisms of early drafts offered by Peter Baehr, Jacques Fomerand, Dennis Dijkzeul, and the editors of this series, especially Tom Weiss. Their encouragement helped me both with content and with the excruciating process of compressing a vast amount of information and theorizing into a short account. The Center of International Studies, now succeeded by the Princeton Institute for International and Regional Studies, and the Department of Politics at Princeton University also offered assistance.

I offer special acknowledgement for helping maintain my morale, a necessary support for a veteran supposedly in retirement, to my daughter, Emilie Gordenker, and to my friend, Sophia Smitskamp.

L.G.

Princeton, NJ, February 2005

1 Introduction

Around the rim of the horse-shoe-shaped table of the United Nations Security Council, imaged in countless television broadcasts, 15 blue-and-white signs identify the representatives of governments. A sixteenth is exceptional. It names no state but only "Secretary-General". He – so far only men have held the post – takes his place with ambassadors, including those of the five permanent Council members whose assent or acquiescence is essential to any important decision, including his appointment. But the Secretary-General speaks, when the President of the Council gives him the floor, only for himself and his staff. He cannot call on a distant capital for the political advantages of an elaborate state apparatus that directs citizens, controls a mighty armed force, a police corps, an intelligence bureau, a tax system, a currency, and the rest of the tools of government. His staff – the UN Secretariat – is hardly numerous enough to man the foreign office of a developed country of modest rank.

Yet the Secretary-General sits with the voting members of a council that on occasion calls down military punishment on offenders against the peace, acts to halt crimes against humanity and offers conciliation in cases of threats of war. He can propose crucial agenda items and offer his views. His position ensures that many governments, usually some important ones, will seriously consider what he has to say. His staff members work with every one of the numerous organs and sub-organs of an organization with a truly global agenda. Like their chief, they pledge to act for no single government but the collective will of all that are UN members.

In important respects, the Secretary-General and the Secretariat occupy a unique place in international relations. When their posts were created during the planning, discussion and eventual adoption of the UN Charter in the spring of 1945 at the UN Conference on International Organization in San Francisco, its novel elements stood out against the background of World War II. Yet the representatives of 50 governments then might just as easily have emphasized the elements of continuity embodied in the office. Their agreement with the document, however, was formally evidenced on 24 October 1945, when the required number of ratifications brought it into force.[1]

Since then, the scope and practice of the office of Secretary-General has waxed and waned in response to developments in the broader waves of international relations. By the dusk of the twentieth century, the seven men appointed came from different lands and cultures and brought varied experiences to the office. Their work sometimes was signaled with jubilation, sometimes with denigration by governments and even broader sweeps of popular opinion. But the Secretary-General and the Secretariat were never either altogether out of sight or without critics. At all times, they constituted the continuity of the organization in contrast to the periodic proceedings of the inter-governmental organs of the UN structure. Indeed, after the end of the Cold War, the chief UN official and his staff took on an unusual prominence in the Western countries, while in the developing world they continued their earlier on-the-ground activity.

Apart from institutional position, continued visibility derives from the duty of the Secretary-General to report to the UN deliberative organs on the state of world politics. These reports refer to controversies, cooperation and progress or lack of it towards goals set out in the UN Charter. The texts signed by the Secretary-General provide to an often – perhaps usually – inattentive broad public the prodding of a global conscience. It sketches a more detached, if sometimes cryptic, analysis than diplomats representing governments could publish. Combined with what they can propose, it forms the basis of global policy – or at least policy that governments say they would carry out. Beyond that, it reflects the acting UN that may frequently contrast with the quarrelsome intergovernmental UN.

While mass media concentrate on the drama of peace and security, after all the paramount aim of the United Nations, the Secretary-General and the Secretariat receive instructions from the inter-governmental organs to carry out a vast set of tasks. From the annual sessions of the General Assembly, in which all of the 191 UN members states have an equal voice, emanate decisions on nearly 200 agenda items. Some of these represent long-standing concerns, such as the division of Cyprus, while others mirror recent issues, such as the AIDS pandemic. Some are hardly more than trivial. But all signify assigned work for the Secretariat under the overall direction of the Secretary-General, rather than only the deliberative aspects.

Their tasks vary from the obvious housekeeping duties of getting the Council chambers in order for meetings and providing interpretation of speeches and translation of documents submitted by governments to the staging of congresses of thousands of participants. More influential in the formation of policy is the constant flow of paper that records discussions, sets out information for debates, reports on past work, analyzes proposed operations, provides statistical data, and much more. If the Security Council acts mainly to cope with crucial short-term troubles, the rest of the UN organization concentrates on primarily long-term issues and continuing projects. This includes the promotion and protection of human rights; economic development; guarding the environment; social protection and improvement for the world's people; the building of international law; research to improve policies; and a growing list of field operations that includes the control of HIV/AIDS, and the direction of military forces engaged in peace-keeping. Nevertheless, most of the policies adopted by UN organs recommend, or sometimes in the case of the Security Council order, actions by administrative apparatuses directed solely by national governments. The UN mechanisms, including the Secretary-General, may offer substantial help to those governments that want it but must depend in the end on state apparatuses, not on the Secretariat.

What follows in this volume sets out the functions of the UN Secretary-General and Secretariat, their potentialities and limitations, their accomplishments and failures. While probably no general theory exists to bring satisfactory explanatory order to the multiple political, economic, social, legal, organizational and personal factors that shape the office of Secretary-General and staff, the treatment here will seek to set out plausible propositions as to how and why they exist and operate. In the next chapter, attention will focus on the historical developments and legal provisions that give the office its formal shape and condition its subsequent evolution. The third chapter will consider the Secretary-General as chief executive of the organization and his involvement with management, personnel, and budgeting and finances. Then his work as the constable of world peace and its special limitations will be considered, and the promotion of global welfare, including some illustrations of how operations in this vast area are mounted and carried out. This will be followed by a consideration of public initiatives by the Secretary-General and the function of representing the organization to various publics. A concluding chapter essays some generalizations about the office and its incumbents, including consideration of personal attributes and of the special impact of the United States government.

2 Blueprint and evolution of an international office

Both solemn legal provisions and sometimes spectacular international political jousting explain the presence and actions of the Secretary-General among the representatives of states on the Security Council. Moreover, he personally or members of his staff are omnipresent in the intergovernmental organs and institutions of the UN system. This chapter treats the historical, legal and political foundations of the office, the choice of its occupants, and the organization of the Secretariat. These make up the institutional framework within which the Secretary-General and the Secretariat take decisions and carry out mandates.

Historical roots

Contemporary diplomatic practice has primeval roots in the Westphalia Conferences that ended European religious warfare in the mid-nineteenth century. From that time to ours, most diplomats most of the time are presumed to represent, under instructions, what their own governments decide are national interests in relation to that of another sovereign state. Over the years, especially from the second half of the nineteenth century, an increasing number of international conferences with representation from many states offered a known way of settling broad international questions. These included setting territorial boundaries and formally ending colonial wars, and planning future cooperation on arms control and humanitarian limits on the use of weapons. Alongside the conferences on high politics, a growing list of multilateral conferences treated technical issues, such as controlling epidemic diseases and regulating navigation on major European rivers.[1]

Usually these multilateral conferences received such necessary services as production of documents, recording decisions, and other housekeeping tasks from the civil service of a host country or from an improvised service drawn from several participating states. But the decisions taken at late nineteenth-century conferences to create workable cooperation among national postal services and another to integrate the use of new telegraph services created both permanent organizations and attached civil services to serve periodic gatherings of the states' members.

From the Versailles conference that brought a definitive end to World War I, the first international civil service with global scope emerged in 1919 as an essential part of the League of Nations and the closely associated International Labor Organization (ILO).[2] The promise and travails of those organizations, the most ambitious attempt to that time to foster broad international cooperation and cope with international conflict, later served as experimental data for the foundation of the United Nations.[3] In the League, the Secretary-General organized the staff, was responsible for common services and provided information and reports around which the diplomats representing their own governments framed discussions of issues.[4] These ranged in immediacy and scope from threats of war to the long-term task of assembling statistics and studies on population or drafting law-making conventions to control the international trade in narcotic drugs.

The first Secretary-General of the League was the architect of the special status for the League Secretariat as an international civil service. His blueprint provided that the members of the Secretariat would take instructions only from the Secretary-General, not from any national government. That applied, too, to the Secretary-General who had sole responsibility and accountability for what the Secretariat did. The member governments also agreed that secretariat officials should be paid according to the scales used by the best national civil services. In the jargon of the international civil service, this is referred to as the Nobelmaire principle, attributed to an advisory commission headed by a British peer. Its shadow survives in UN practice. Governments were obliged to keep their hands off the Secretariat, to recognize at least the senior members as diplomatic personnel who were guarded from national jurisdictions in the course of their duties. Nothing as broad as this international status had been provided for earlier intergovernmental organizations.

Even though it was established in great part as the result of American efforts, the United States later refused, after a bitter internal controversy, to join the League of Nations. Nevertheless, the experience of the organization could not be overlooked as a base for postwar planning. Indeed veterans of the League Secretariat, including its first Secretary-General, had offered their reflections in a debate in the

British House of Lords and in studies research organizations in both the United Kingdom and the United States.[5] Designing the United Nations took place mainly in the offices of the United States government. Some input came from Great Britain, but France and China had little role during World War II; the contributions of the Soviet Union affected a few critical political structures only in the final phases, especially as a result of the Yalta Conference. What gelled in the planning process met the obvious need that a continuing global organization would need a secretariat.

The model provided by the League of Nations for the office of Secretary-General had more kinship with the British notion of a civil service that kept to the background, while providing sophisticated advice and necessary services to ministers who were members of parliament, than with the American approach of a government service headed and under the orders of a leading, powerful political official whose status equaled that of the legislature. At the same time, the first Director-General of the ILO, a product of French politics, demonstrated that at least in more defined issues strong executive leadership in international cooperation could be accepted.[6]

UN Charter provisions

The results of planning for the UN Charter, including more specific provisions for a Secretary-General than those for the League, came under decisive scrutiny at the San Francisco Conference. In general, the provisions for the Secretariat and its head met little objection. Clearly the governments that legally committed themselves to postwar international organization accepted that a secretariat would be needed even if its international status caused some suspicion. Nevertheless, the constitutional framework in Chapter XV of the UN Charter establishing the Secretariat has remained unchanged since then.[7]

The Secretariat has the status of one of the five principal organs, along with the intergovernmental Security Council, the General Assembly, the Economic and Social Council (ECOSOC), the Trusteeship Council, as well as the International Court of Justice. The legal significance of this language in Article 7 of the UN Charter has never been very clear, but it does signify that the Secretariat, headed by the Secretary-General, was intended as an important part of the organization and not merely part of the background apparatus or the shy hand-maiden of all work.

Along the lines drawn by the practice of the League of Nations, the UN Charter explicitly promotes the international status of the

Secretary-General and the Secretariat by barring them from seeking or accepting instructions from any government. Article 100 obligates member governments to respect "the exclusively international character of the responsibilities of the Secretary-General and the staff". The governments undertake not "to seek to influence them" in their work.

The other main UN organs, with the exception of the International Court of Justice,[8] are manned by delegates appointed and presumably instructed by their own governments. In contrast, the choice of the Secretary-General is accomplished in two formal steps which together invoke the responsibility of the entire UN membership. To begin with, each member of the Security Council decides who it will take seriously as candidates. One of them will eventually receive the recommendation of the Council, including the necessary support of the permanent members. The nomination then goes to the General Assembly where the entire UN membership decides by a majority vote whether to appoint the recommended candidate. In separate resolutions, the General Assembly has made a practice of appointments for terms of five years and accepts reappointment of an incumbent. The General Assembly also determines the level of pay and perquisites, such as expense allowances, of the office.

The Secretary-General is designated in the UN Charter as the chief administrative officer of the organization.[9] He acts as Secretary-General in other organs of the UN and carries out the functions assigned by them. He is required to make an annual report to the General Assembly.

As chief officer, he is responsible for the appointment of the Secretariat. These appointments are governed by regulations set down by the General Assembly and updated on the basis of proposals mainly by the Secretary-General. Each of the Councils is assigned an appropriate staff which are part of the Secretariat. Article 100 of the Charter includes a statement of the qualifications of the Secretariat members:

> The paramount consideration in the employment of the staff and in the determination of the conditions of service shall be the necessity of securing the highest standards of efficiency, competence, and integrity. Due regard shall be paid to the importance of recruiting ... on as wide a geographical basis as possible.

Beyond these provisions, which mainly establish a formal character for the Secretariat and, by implication, for its chief, and mark out organizational foundations, the Secretary-General is endowed with a quite explicit political capacity that was novel at the end of World War II. This is set out in the single terse sentence of Article 99 of the Charter:

> The Secretary-General may bring to the attention of the Security Council any matter which in his opinion may threaten the maintenance of international peace and security.

Filling out the framework

Constitutional experts long ago concluded that a good legal foundation for a public organization should be short, direct and clear. In many respects the UN Charter matches that requirement, but in the case of the Secretary-General both logic and practice have raised fundamental questions about what is intended, politically possible and desirable.

The queries begin with the appointment process. Who actually proposes candidates and what must their qualifications be? The answer to the second part is simple enough: nobody really knows. The Charter is silent on the matter, except perhaps by implication in the phrase in Article 100 about the highest standards of efficiency, competence and integrity.

As for proposing candidates, clearly that is formally a matter for the Security Council, five of whose members are permanent and the other 10 elected for two-year terms. Any representative on the Security Council could be persuaded by a non-member, a newspaper article, a prior experience, or even a sudden inspiration to put forward a name. More likely, the Council delegates would have directed suggestions to, or heard from, their governments about candidates who would seem to support national aims. Those names might have been proposed to the government by its representative on the Council on the basis of research, impression, whim, or horse-trading. The veto-armed Permanent Five can stop the nomination of any candidate for any reason; under Council practice, their negotiations take place in secret before a public vote. They are not obliged to explain secret opposition although eventual leaks and the public voting session provide some clarity. Whatever the case, the Security Council has never developed a systematic search mechanism that would encourage excellent appointments in every case. Rather, the "search for the best person for what is one of the world's most important office has … become a chancy and, to some extent, self-serving process".[10]

Biographies of Secretaries-General

Trygve Lie (1896-1968)

Born Oslo. Degree in law, Oslo University. Legal adviser to Trade Union Federation, 1922-35. Minister of Justice,1935-39. Minister of Trade, Industry, Shipping and Fishing, 1939-40. Escaped to England to join government in exile. Minister of Foreign Affairs, 1941-45. Chairman, Norwegian delegation to San Francisco Conference, 1945. Secretary-General, 1946-53.

Dag Hammarskjöld (1905-1961)

Born Jonkoping, Sweden. Degrees in economics, law and social philosophy, Uppsala University and Stockholm University. Permanent Under-secretary, Ministry of Finance, 1936-45. Chairman, National Bank Board, 1941-48. Under-secretary, Foreign Office, 1947-49. Secretary-General, Foreign Office, 1949-51. Minister without Portfolio, 1951-53. Member, Swedish Academy, 1954. Secretary-General, 1953-1961.

U Thant (1909-74)

Born Pantanaw, Burma. Teacher training, University College, Rangoon. Headmaster, Pantanaw High School, 1931, 1943-47. Freelance journalist. Secretary, Ministry of Information, 1949-57. Representative to UN, 1957-61. Acting UN Secretary-General, 1962-63. Secretary-General, 1964-71.

Kurt Waldheim (1918-)

Born Vienna. German army, 1939-42. Degree in law, University of Vienna. Austrian foreign service, 1945-64. Representative to UN, 1964-68. Foreign minister, 1968-70. Unsuccessful candidate for president, 1971. Secretary-General, 1972-92. President of Austria, 1986-.

Javier Pérez de Cuéllar (1920-)

Born Lima, Peru. Degree in law, Catholic University, Lima. Peruvian foreign ministry and diplomatic service, 1940-74. Representative to UN, 1971-75. UN Special Representative in

Cyprus, 1975-77. UN Under-Secretary-General, 1979-81. Secretary-General, 1982-91. Prime Minister, 2000-1. Ambassador to France, 2001-.

Boutros Boutros-Ghali (1922-)
   Born Cairo. Degree in law, Cairo University, PhD, Paris. Professor, Cairo University, 1949-77. Minister of State for Foreign Affairs, 1977-91. Deputy foreign minister, 1991-92. Secretary-General, 1992-96. Secretary-General, Organisation Internationale de la Francophonie, 1997-2002.

Kofi A. Annan (1938-)
   Born Kumasi, Ghana. Degree in economics, Macalester College, further studies at Graduate Institute of International Studies, Geneva, and Massachusetts Institute of Technology. World Health Organization secretariat, 1962-71. UN Secretariat, Geneva and New York, 1972-; Under-Secretary-General, 1993-96. Secretary-General, 1997-.

The history of the appointments suggests a few familiar routes. All but one of the Secretaries-General served a national government in a senior foreign affairs post. The one exception, Kofi Annan, had a career in the Secretariat that brought him into close contact with governmental representatives on matters of peace and security. All were nationals of governments other than the Permanent Five of the Security Council. Two were Scandinavians and three from developing countries. Only one came from Asia and two from Africa. All had enthusiastic backing of the government of their country of origin. The record suggests a strong preference among the majority of governments for a kind of rotation and balance among regions and an exclusion of candidates from permanent members of the Security Council and large powerful states. If this holds, the next Secretary-General would come from a small Asian country.

   One other factor figured strongly in each appointment. Broadly speaking, that could be labeled as international politics in which the Permanent Members of the Security Council took determining positions. Some illustrations make this clear.[11]

   The first Secretary-General, Trygve Lie, had been wartime foreign minister of the Norwegian government in exile in London. The hardening antagonism of the Soviet Union and the United States excluded candidates from most of Western Europe and North America, the obvious places to look in 1945. But Lie, a veteran trade union lawyer, had a name for enough political leaning to the left to be acceptable to Moscow and enough obscurity to pass through American filters. In any case, the dimensions of the post were unknown and the presidency of the General Assembly was then thought to be perhaps more important.

Lie almost inevitably developed enemies as he tried out the limits of his new job, which included organizing the Secretariat, setting up a permanent headquarters in the United States, dealing with the Security Council and escaping as far as possible from the grinding effect of the Cold War. Above all, it was the last that cost him reappointment, for the Soviet Union denounced his public approval of the action of the Security Council to act militarily against the North Korean attack on South Korea in 1950. From that point on, Moscow refused all contact with Lie and vetoed his reappointment. Despite strident Soviet objections, the General Assembly simply extended his term of office. Lie resigned in 1953, bitterly stating that Soviet opposition meant he could no longer work effectively.[12]

Dag Hammarskjöld, the second Secretary-General, who had had a brilliant career, including high rank in the Swedish foreign ministry, apparently seemed a safe, pacifying bet to the Security Council. His candidature was suggested by the French government, whose officials knew him as an outstanding bureaucrat in the context of European economic cooperation. His prominence as a peacekeeper, as well as his expansion of the scope of his office, was unexpected and eventually led to another spectacular incident of Soviet opposition in the context of the Cold War. Moscow accused him of partisanship in his direction of the vast UN mission, approved by the Security Council, after the implosion of the new state of the Congo in 1960 (see Chapter 4). Hammarskjöld died in an aircraft accident in 1961, obviating the question of his reappointment. The Soviet Union had proclaimed it would oppose Hammarskjöld's candidacy and without success insisted that the office ought to be changed into a three-headed committee, famed at the time as a "Troika" (a Russian sleigh drawn by three horses).[13]

U Thant, the third Secretary-General, took office in 1962 as Acting Secretary-General, in the shadow of the Troika idea, which the USSR still promoted. At the time, he was the permanent representative of Burma to the UN, and obscure to most publics beyond the diplomatic circle. After a good deal of background bargaining, Thant passed through the East–West sieve and eventually was appointed to full rank, whereupon he promptly signaled that he favored the same independence that his predecessors claimed. He played a significant role in cooling the Cuban missile crisis of 1961. He pleaded for more attention to the needs of the developing world, and behind the scenes as well as in speeches tried to promote a settlement of the Viet Nam war, which had never engaged the Security Council. His opposition to the American policy on Viet Nam won him little regard from the Johnson administration. Because of illness, he declined to be considered for yet another term.[14]

Kurt Waldheim, the fourth Secretary-General, then the foreign minister of Austria and former permanent representative in New York, was well-known in diplomatic circles as a competent, if not brilliant, operator. He passed through the Security Council without special opposition from either East or West and served out two terms at a time when his organization went through a rather indifferent period. He assiduously promoted the idea that the Secretary-General should have an important role in broad international negotiations, such as those on the Israeli–Palestinian dispute, but had little decisive effect. He failed in an obvious bid to be appointed to a third term. He then was elected president of Austria in a campaign that raised questions of his wartime record, especially possible participation in Nazi outrages in Yugoslavia.[15]

Javier Pérez de Cuéllar, the fifth Secretary-General, served as permanent representative of Peru to the UN at the time of his appointment. While he had strong backing from his government and much of the Latin American group, which considered it high time that it successfully sponsored a candidate, he was widely thought to represent a calm approach to the office. He readily obtained the recommendation of the Permanent Five, perhaps because they expected little of him.[16] In his two terms of office, he concentrated on behind-the-scenes diplomacy that had a significant effect in reducing strife in Central America, especially in El Salvador and Nicaragua. He presided over the Secretariat and adapted his views to hail the end of the Cold War. He did not put himself forward for a third term.

Boutros Boutros-Ghali, the sixth Secretary-General, sometime deputy foreign minister of Egypt and special adviser to the President, was the first open, energetic campaigner for the office. Experienced through an unsuccessful drive to become Director-General of the UN Educational, Scientific and Cultural Organization (UNESCO), Boutros-Ghali had strong backing from his government and stimulated support from the numerous African group as the first candidate from that continent. He drove through a quick reorganization of the Secretariat, stressing economy and efficiency. Having promised to serve for only one term, he changed his mind, but encountered open, heavy, and sometimes ludicrous opposition from the United States government, as well as much congressional and popular opinion. The Security Council resolution on his reappointment was opposed only by the United States which vetoed his candidacy.[17]

Kofi Annan, the seventh Secretary-General, also had wide support from the African group, his native Ghana and growing enthusiasm on the part of the United States. The rest of the Security Council, which had supported Boutros-Ghali, went along with Annan's appointment, not only because of American and African pressure but also because they knew him as an experienced international civil servant of integrity and dependability. He was reappointed ahead of schedule to a second term as a result of wide satisfaction with his program of reform of the Secretariat and his adroit diplomatic performance.

Once a Secretary-General is chosen, he invariably feels the tension inherent even in the bare language of the Charter. He is the Secretary-General of every organ: therefore he provides them with the usual housekeeping services as well as reports that may propose policies and indicate the progress of approved programs. Yet he carries out the instructions adopted by the other organs. At the same time, he or his staff members sit alongside national delegates in the meetings of the organs they serve. The implications of the Charter provisions underline the expectation that his views and proposals will be taken seriously. They may lead to instructions that put him at the head of programs of worldwide renown or notoriety. Nevertheless, such instructions ultimately must have support of governments that he may sometimes persuade but never actually direct. Moreover, when other organizations of the UN system are involved, he may at best function as the most distinguished among peers (see Chapter 5). Thus is posed the unrelenting question as to whether the Secretary-General is merely a servant or primarily a commander.

The Secretariat and the Secretary-General

The provisions of the Charter appear to endow the Secretary-General with virtually complete command over the Secretariat, bound only by the high qualifications for the appointment of its members. But practice builds a rather more limited chief administrative office than might be imagined from the title.

From the beginning of the organization, the Permanent Five of the Security Council reached a private agreement that diminishes the international character of the Secretariat. They agreed that they each would nominate candidates who would be appointed to the second rank immediately below the Secretary-General.[18] This meant that the Secretary-General could not fully carry out the provision of Article 101 that appointments should be made on the basis of "the highest standards of efficiency, competence and integrity." Instead he could apply these standards only to names – in the case of the Soviet Union, sometimes one name – put to him by the Permanent Five as possible top-rank officials. In the case of the initial design of the Secretariat, proposed by Trygve Lie, eight Assistant Secretaries-General were to be named: five of them were nominated by the Permanent Five. This route of nomination has never been abandoned. The top-level of the Secretariat always includes, for better or worse, nationals of the Permanent Five.

This practice immediately raises the question as to whether officials so nominated to top positions in the Secretariat can remain impartial in the face of pressures from their own governments. It also violates the logic of an international civil service which is supposed to serve only the United Nations, not particular governments.

The question also is raised again in applying the injunction to make appointments that give due regard to "as wide a geographical basis as possible". Does this mean that the national source of candidate for appointment is just as important as efficiency, competence and integrity? If not, then what is the appropriate balance? Or is it not a question of balance but rather of an overriding set of qualifications?

In any case, Article 101 states that staff appointments are to be made according to regulations established by the General Assembly. Such regulations do not spontaneously appear. In fact, the first Secretary-General, acting on advice from an intergovernmental group of consultants, proposed the staff rules. These were in part based on the experience of the League of Nations and in part on what were considered good ideas for managing a public service with pioneering tasks.[19] While initially the rules were adopted without much friction, later the General Assembly at times proved perfectly willing to interfere with the Secretary-General's idea of how appointments should be made (see Chapter 3).[20]

The legal structure of the office of the Secretary-General and the Secretariat, as well as rules and practices adopted by the other organs, includes opportunities for differing applications. The resulting chances to extend national aims into the international civil service were anything but neglected by the UN members. The next chapter takes up how the Secretary-General manages the Secretariat and how international politics shapes his policies.

3 The UN Secretariat and its responsible chief

If the hand of the Secretary-General is expected, as the UN Charter directs or implies, to be omnipresent in the organization and even to take policy initiatives, he obviously needs a staff. That and diplomatic needs dictate the establishment of the Secretariat. But it settles neither the issue of the size, its form, or precisely what it does. Here the hierarchical organizational model suggested in the Charter both instructs and misleads.

An unadulterated version of the Secretary-General as chief officer would allow him to put together the Secretariat with only general policy collaboration from a superior organ, in this case the General Assembly. He would have very broad organizational powers uninhibited by backroom deals and micromanagement from outside. He would bear responsibility for what was done and would expect to account to the organ that approves overall policy. In many respects, this model suggests a utopian snapshot of the American presidential system. It differs, for instance, from the Western European cabinet form in which cabinet ministers are drawn from the leading parties in the legislature.

Neither the presidential nor the cabinet version fits with either the history or the complexity of UN tasks undertaken during more than five decades. Both the work of the Secretary-General and the profile of the Secretariat have constantly been shaped by political forces contending inside the UN organs and sometimes deep within member governments. This chapter sets out the current organization of the Secretariat and, while noting its development, links it with internal initiatives by the Secretary-General (see further discussion in Chapter 6, below), explores the crucial budgeting and financing process, and along the way offer some glimpses of what the Secretariat does.

Oiling the international gears

While the notion of a permanent secretariat for an international organization has a short history, diplomatic practice and the League of Nations provided substantial guides. In both cases, the gathering of representatives of governments required technical and housekeeping services that had to be furnished by civil servants, but the League and a handful of other bodies made the concept of a permanent *international* service familiar.

The UN Secretariat is expected flawlessly to furnish the needed services to the General Assembly, the Security Council and other organs routinely and dependably. They constitute a necessary lubricant in international machinery as well as an indispensable memory. They also result in continuing overhead costs.

The UN Secretariat includes a Department for General Assembly and Conference Management to provide these basic services which are anything but simple to organize and staff. The UN operates on six official languages – Arabic, Chinese, English, French, Russian and Spanish – of which English and French are working languages. Arabic was added in 1975 to the original five languages in response to pressure from governments of countries that use it. In practice this demands official records produced in all official languages, interpretation for them in main organs and some others, a flow of edited documents needed for meetings in at least the working languages and printed and electronic publication of documentary collections to aid discourse.

The organizational map of the General Assembly, the largest of the main organs that brings together representatives of all 191 member states at least once a year, makes clear how extensive is the inherent demand for services. As of 2003, the Secretariat provided necessary services for six main committees on which all members of the General Assembly are represented, two procedural committees, two standing committees, 16 intergovernmental bodies of various membership, four *ad hoc* open-ended (any government may join) working groups, two advisory bodies and nine bodies consisting of experts. Either the Secretary-General or an authorized representative must be present for almost all of the meetings to advise the chair and, when asked, to speak and explain existing policies and practices. During sessions, proposals by governments and reports by the Secretariat or intergovernmental bodies on assigned work have to be edited, translated, reproduced, circulated and decisions recorded, circulated and preserved for the next session. Incidentally, most such documentation is readily available electronically via the UN internet site: http://www.un.org (see Chapter 6 below for discussion).

The General Assembly in 2003 dealt with 671 documents, ranging from one paragraph to several hundred pages, not counting drafts and memoranda that do not enter the permanent record. These formal documents include reports by the Secretary-General, obviously prepared by specialized parts of the staff, on some items that have been on the agenda for more than half a century, such as aspects of the situation in the Middle East. Others deal with new items suggested by UN members. A large handful of the documents lay out in exquisite detail but not always political precision the budgetary, personnel and organizational matters on which the General Assembly has the last word.

A document that sometimes has had special significance is the *Annual Report of the Secretary-General on the Work of the Organization* which meets a requirement of the UN Charter. Some of the Secretaries-General have made this a vehicle for analysis of the state of international relations generally and of what the organization contributes and where it may fall short. Other Secretaries-General, including Annan, simply report in a brief manner on every program assigned to the Secretariat. In any case, much of the report is made up of contributions from the various departments of the Secretariat. These are edited in the Secretary-General's office into final form. Whether or not the *Annual Report* forms a nucleus for discussion in the General Assembly and elsewhere depends on the always disparate reactions of the representatives of member governments.

Aside from the General Assembly structure, the Security Council and ECOSOC also require services. (Earlier, before the handful of Trust Territories gained independence, the Trusteeship Council, which is now practically moribund, required similar services.) They too establish sub-organs. Because ECOSOC involves complicated and novel issues extending over long time-periods, its structure includes advisory bodies, intergovernmental committees, and organs to provide contact with other international and non-governmental organizations.

The work of ECOSOC (taken up in more detail in Chapter 5) justifies a global statistical service whose publications form the basis not only of international policy but also that of national governments, other international organizations, and private businesses. A thick statistical yearbook, covering country-by-country such topics as population, measures of economic development, tourism, and much more, collects the output of all governments and benefits from continuous expert consultation. More specialized statistical publications, such as a demographic yearbook, provides detailed background for other agenda items. To such publications are added specific forward-looking Secretariat studies and statistics on long-term issues, such as control of narcotic drugs and appropriate approaches to economic development, made in response to orders from ECOSOC and the General Assembly. This material is covered in a more general way, along with developments in the field of peace-maintenance and the growth of international law, in the massive *Yearbook of the United Nations*, produced by the Department of Public Information (see Chapter 6). All of these publications depend on compiling and editing services performed by the Secretariat.

Some of the Secretariat operations reach far and wide in issues of global governance, that is the creation of consensual policies to regulate international relations. It has, for instance, prepared the groundwork for vast transnational conferences on population, on the status of women, on human rights and on the environment.[1] The end product of such conferences is usually a document setting out the undertakings that most governments in the world approve to deal with such global issues. The member governments, in any case, decide for themselves whether to oblige their administrations and their nationals to put the global policies in effect. In order to define the subject matter and develop recommendations, the Secretariat consults and orders studies by experts and professional associations in many countries, convenes preparatory committees to refine the findings, and prepares the documentation. Then it manages the services for the meetings which are usually held away from the main UN offices in New York, Geneva and Vienna in order to get closer to different populations. Such events attract representatives, as many as tens of thousands, from non-governmental organizations (NGOs) with which the Secretariat maintains close liaison. Until the final phase of approving the concluding intergovernmental declaration, this sort of operation differs sharply from usual diplomatic practice and has increasingly involved the Secretariat with broader constituencies.

In the case of the Security Council, the Secretary-General himself is usually present, both in public sessions and in private discussions with representatives of governments (see Chapter 4 for discussion). Here, too, a steady flow of documents is required, including many detailed reports from the Secretary-General, based on missions to the places where disturbances to the peace need remedies. Such documents as these usually contain diplomatic or cryptic judgments by the Secretariat and its chief of developments on such sensitive assignments as the strife and ultimate genocide in Rwanda in the 1990s or the humanitarian disaster of Darfur, Sudan, in 2004. In the Rwanda instance, Secretary-General Annan later submitted an unusually critical retrospective analysis of the acknowledged failure of the UN machinery to prevent effectively the mass slaughter and subsequent disturbance of the peace in the surrounding countries.[2]

Organizing a bureaucracy

Even demands for routine services inevitably give birth to a standing bureaucracy[3] – in this case the Secretariat. The Secretary-General bears the burden of organizing this international staff that despite formal shielding feels the buffeting of international politics. His mandate includes finding staff members who not only meet high standards but also match in some way the geographical spread of the member states. At the same time, the staff must perform duties given it by the Secretary-General and other organs efficiently, remain independent of governments, and ultimately satisfy the UN members during deliberations of the General Assembly and outside it.

Exactly what comprises the UN Secretariat requires definition. Formally it includes the staffs of autonomous organs created by the General Assembly, such as the UN Development Programme, the UN Children's Fund, the UN Environmental Programme and the UN University which have their own memberships, directing councils and financial contributors. Adding everything together, the international civil service that is associated with some oversight by the General Assembly, consists of somewhat more than 25,000 persons, plus some extra personnel on short-term (it is hoped) political and peace maintenance missions of various sizes. While a common set of staff rules governs all of this international staff, the core UN staff consists of about 9,000 persons who are paid out of the appropriations approved by the General Assembly. This total does not include the sometimes sizable military field missions to maintain peace. And the staff members of such specialized agencies as ILO and the World Bank also do not count as UN Secretariat. If the numbers of all the international civil servants associated with the UN system were summed up, they would come to about 50,000, scattered in many locations.

While the New York headquarters is home to the core, some officials are assigned to the five regional economic and social commissions and to the offices in Geneva, Nairobi and Vienna. The entire staff, moreover, is divided into those who are mainly nationals of the host government of a duty station and locally appointed, and the international recruits who hold professional posts and get most political attention.

The international character of the staff and the independence of the Secretary-General was diluted from the beginning by actions of member governments. The still-applied authority-sapping "gentleman's agreement" of 1945, on appointments to the level immediately below the Secretary-General anticipated the deepening Cold War (see Chapter 2 above). It also provided an escape from Soviet demands that the Secretariat should be exclusively organized around the principal organs so that, for example, the Security Council would have its own exclusive staff, presumably not under the Secretary-General's control. It rejected, too, the notions of some other governments that the General Assembly should appoint the second-level Secretariat officials.

Consequently, the first Secretary-General, Trygve Lie, established eight departments in the Secretariat, three of them specializing in the work of the three major councils and a legal department; the rest either were charged with internal tasks or public relations.[4] One of the latter went to the United States, which selected a nominee for the administrative and budgetary department, presumably because its functions gave Washington an overview and voice in everything that would happen in the staff.

This pattern – specialization in subject matter or in overall services – provided the main organizational concept until 1997, when Secretary-General Kofi Annan undertook a major reorganization (which will be described below). Each Secretary-General, however, had added to or altered the general concept to conform to his preferences and to react to political pressures from member governments. For instance, during Waldheim's tenure an intensive, rather controversial, organizational study by a committee appointed by the General Assembly led to some changes. Under strong pressure from financial shortfalls and pressure from the wealthy governments, especially the United States, Boutros-Ghali "delegated and decentralized the system by stopping the practice of having dozens of top officials report directly to [him]. Other reforms aimed to reduce budgetary staff levels.".[5] He combined six existing departments, each headed by a senior official, into one Department of Political Affairs, and abolished 18 high-ranking jobs, including a supreme economic post originally intended to affect the entire secretariat. A department to oversee humanitarian activities, such as disaster relief, was organized. During his tenure, the United States insisted on the addition of a ranking official and a small department, designated as the Office of Internal Oversight Services, to function as an autonomous inspector-general of the Secretariat.

As the UN agenda expands to reflect growing complexities in what governments deemed useful for international treatment, duties and new topics are distributed among the departments.[6] None of the Secretaries-General, however, ever used the second-level officials, titled as Under-Secretary-General or Assistant Secretary-General,[7] as a cabinet that systematically studied and supported important decisions. Nor was there a fixed arrangement for a deputy who would take over the direction in the absence or illness of the chief.

A reorganization undertaken by Annan included the proposal of an office of Deputy Secretary-General to bear some of the management and representational burden associated with his office. The General Assembly accepted this move and Annan appointed Louise Fréchette, a Canadian national, to the post. In order to give shape to the development and assessment of policies, Annan established two levels of consultative committees which substitute a more collective, organized style of reaching decisions for the earlier less systematic practice of managing programs. These comprise a Senior Management Group and, below that in rank, a set of Executive Committees.

The Senior Management Group includes all officials of the Under-Secretary-General or Assistant Secretary-General rank, including the Legal Adviser. These are the heads of the departments and offices of the Secretariat as well as the heads of largely autonomous agencies created by the General Assembly. The Group meets weekly with the Secretary-General or the Deputy Secretary-General in the chair. A teleconferencing connection provides access for the senior UN officials in Geneva, including the heads of the Geneva and Vienna offices, the UN Commissioner for Human Rights (UNCHR), and the UN High Commissioner for Refugees (UNHCR). In rotation, the chief officers of the five UN regional economic and social commissions join. Usually each meeting has a theme or central agenda which is supported by a staff paper. Discussions are directed to clarifying issues and options, exchanging information, and decisions on the spot by the Secretary-General as to which departments should act. A few subjects, such as the conflicts involving Israel, are considered so politically loaded as to require special confidentiality and direct participation exclusively by the Secretary-General and his immediate executive office.

The four Executive Committees take specific functional areas as their province. These include economic development, peace and security, humanitarian services, and global economic and social issues. These committees include the directors of programs and other concerned officials who have active projects in these sectors. The primary output of these committees is coordination and mutual information rather than decisions. They reflect the complex implications of global issues, such as economic development, which do not fit tidily within specialized administrative bureaus.

The Secretary-General's office also includes a strategic planning unit and several advisers who have special assignments, such as the

UN Secretariat: Departments and Offices

Secretary-General
Office of the Secretary-General
Office of Internal Oversight Services
Office of Legal Affairs
Department of Political Affairs
Department for Disarmament Affairs
Department of Peacekeeping Operations
Office for the Coordination of Humanitarian Affairs
Department of Economic and Social Affairs
Department for General Assembly and Conference Management
Department of Public Information
Department of Management
Office of the Iraq Programme
Office of the High Representative for the Least Developed Countries, Landlocked Developing Countries and Small Island Developing States
Office on Drugs and Crime
Office of the UN Security Coordinator
UN Office at Geneva
UN Office at Vienna
UN Office at Nairobi

Source: UN Press Release DPI, March 2004

global campaign against AIDS, and the drafting of speeches and statements. Although the organized bureaucratic committees and task forces for special projects spread far and wide over global concerns, nevertheless they are primarily concerned with policy rather than managing the output of products or services going directly to consumers. Therefore, the question of how member governments will receive proposed policies, whether they will undertake their execution and how the results will be judged adds a political dimension to every proposal, decision or review. Whether the Annan model or another guides relations at the top of the Secretariat, managing and fitting together the flow from inside and outwards of information about forming and carrying out policy is a primary aim.

Personnel

As in all organizations, at the heart of internal housekeeping in the United Nations lie recruiting, appointing and assigning personnel. How to go about accomplishing this task in the framework of an international civil service poses difficulties that have affected each Secretary-General and which find resonance in national politics.

The term "civil service" implies a merit-based, permanent corps of functionaries most of whom begin their careers as juniors in the hierarchy and advance to higher positions on the basis of their performance and seniority . Such civil servants receive assignments to a department on the basis of existing specialization or as recruits expected to serve a kind of apprenticeship, learning and rising in authority. The UN Charter, as noted, fills in this structural concept with a qualitative standard of high efficiency and integrity and a second one of wide representation of national origins of Secretariat members.

The top-level UN appointments do not conform to the civil service model of continuous service and advancement on the basis of performance. That is guaranteed by the "gentleman's agreement" among the permanent members of the Security Council and resembles the practice at the political level in many governments. The exceptions are further extended by the creation, under the authority of the General Assembly, of largely autonomous organizations within the UN system, such as the UN Development Programme. Here the Secretary-General appoints the heads, usually with the concurrence of the General Assembly and consultations with governments that do not hesitate to make strong suggestions. The organizational heads rank as Under-Secretaries-General. Yet once appointed, these officials manage their own specific organizational and personnel issues under general UN civil service regulations. Within their organizations, like all intergovernmental bodies, including NATO and the European Union, the distribution of top jobs among the leading governments raises a continuing issue.

Given the global UN membership, the search for recruits to the Secretariat should suffer from no shortage of candidates. Indeed that is so, as each year thousands apply for jobs. Yet the professional ranks – in UN jargon, those subject to desirable ranges of geographical distribution – include only some 4,000 posts. The paucity of staff and lack of financing, aside from technical issues, work contrary to a general system of examinations or even a serious reading of most of the applications. Rather, the Secretary-General and his personnel staff mainly rely on suggestions from the member governments, especially for openings at the higher ranks. Nevertheless, a beginning has been made on an examination system, operated by a few governments, to identify candidates who might be chosen for the entry levels of the professional cadre.

Most delegations to the UN show strong interest in the higher ranks of the international civil service. "Here", wrote Waldheim, "I regret to say, political pressures have become all too common".[8] Exactly why any government wants as many of its nationals as it can place in the Secretariat is not always clear. "A senior UN official nominated by his or her government was ... assumed to be in the Secretariat to do that government's bidding; this assumption was not always right but it could position relations within the Secretariat", according to former Under-Secretary-General Marrack Goulding.[9]

Among the reasons usually given for pressure by governments for appointments are: ease of contact with work in progress; presence of persons to explain a particular culture or regional experience; avoiding domination by any one political or cultural tendency; a just distribution according to the contributions each government pays; recognizing national political support; and providing an outstanding servant for an open post. These rather anodyne justifications for suggesting candidates can be offset against some reasons that are rarely openly admitted: capping a diplomatic career with an attractive post in New York, Geneva or Vienna; getting out from under a dictatorial regime; a successful ploy for getting rid of a now useless national servant or politician; providing for a feckless relative; waiting with a good salary until a better post in a national service comes free; spying;[10] rewards by the home government for good service in otherwise nasty circumstances; rescuing a colleague from a national "reduction-in-force"; and just plainly getting a better salary than the home economy offers. Insiders in the Secretariat whisper about matches among their colleagues for each of these reasons.

Ultimately the Secretary-General must make a choice among the candidates which governments suggest for middle-level posts upwards, the candidates from the existing staff, and those suggested by experts inside and out who may be consulted. Some governments leave the Secretariat little choice. For 33 years ending in 1986, the United States presented to the UN conclusions of its time-consuming investigations of the loyalty to itself of candidates of American nationality; the clear implication was that the Secretary-General would do well to ignore certain candidates and respond favorably to nominations. Some, probably few, governments with a more collegial attitudes offer outstanding candidates for appointment. In addition, the Charter sets gender equality as a purpose.[11] The General Assembly urges this as a standard, along with no discrimination because of age for Secretariat appointments (retirement for new recruits is at age 62), even if many governments neglect it at home. In any case, the appointments process involves dangerous political traps for the Secretary-General.

The General Assembly has assiduously complicated the appointments process by setting geographical targets for the manning of the professional ranks of the Secretariat.[12] In principle, each of the 191 UN members has the right to expect at least one or two of its nationals will serve on the UN Secretariat. Members that make large contributions to the UN budget or that have large populations get a larger range of appointments. Nevertheless, the organization must have a solid core of able civil servants. Persons with the relevant experience and training can more easily be found in rich countries than elsewhere. Consequently, the number of appointees from rich countries in the West tends to reach beyond the upper edges of the range. So do those of a few very populous developing countries, such as India, that have stocks of highly-educated persons working in large civil services. Nationals of the United States, however, have in recent years not numbered enough to come very high in, and sometimes fall below, the desired range prescribed by the General Assembly. In this regard, among the explanations that have been alleged are the unpopularity of the organization in some political circles in Washington; the level of salaries which are below the private sector in the United States (as are those of the American civil service); the accent on recruitment from developing and new member countries; and procedures of recruitment that seem cumbersome and opaque to American candidates. At the same time, a large proportion of the local (not international) recruits employed in New York are nationals of the United States.

What in practice are trade unions of international civil servants affect the management of the Secretariat. Their ultimate weapon of strikes has only rarely been used and never on a system-wide basis. Rather, senior management officials, and sometimes the Secretary-General, carry on discussions with them involving such topics as salary levels, home leave provisions, claims of arbitrary dismissal, security and safety while on missions, and procedures for promotion. On the whole, these issues have a mirror image in many national civil services.

Another protection for the staff is the independent UN Administrative Tribunal that decides on the merits of legal complaints by Secretariat members of violations of the staff rules, such as unwarranted dismissal. More generally, an International Civil Service Commission, appointed by the General Assembly, offers advice on procedures and rules for the entire UN system.

The real quality of the Secretariat cannot be read out of these complications. Most of them reflect the unwillingness of the governments to persuade themselves and their colleagues in the General Assembly that a protected international civil service bears importantly on their concerns and leaves the autonomy of their states in place.

Out of the tangle of constraints, rules and meddling, some figures of global importance have emerged. Annan, in the post of Secretary-General, offers a paramount example. He began as a junior official and eventually became the first Secretariat member to reach the highest office. He and the organization were awarded the Nobel Peace Prize. One of his highly esteemed lieutenants, Sergio Vieira de Mello, a Brazilian who had overseen the nation-forming mission in East Timor and was serving as High Commissioner for Human Rights, was killed in the UN office he directed in Baghdad in 2003, in an attack that also claimed other UN staffers and NGO officials; the Brazilian government was saddened enough to proclaim a time of national mourning. Earlier, Ralph Bunche, an American,[13] won the Nobel Peace Prize for his work in setting up the armistice in 1949 between Israel and its neighbors that provided some structure for seeking peace during the next half century. Dag Hammarskjöld was posthumously awarded the Nobel Peace Prize in 1961. The Swedish social scientist, Gunnar Myrdal, who was serving as executive secretary of the UN Economic Commission for Europe, won the Nobel Prize for Economics in 1974. In the 1990s, the UN peacekeepers as a body won the Nobel Peace Prize. Other Secretariat members have advanced economic thought,[14] have produced meticulous statistical studies that the entire world uses, and have augmented international jurisprudence. Most labor unsung, some of them in harsh conditions in which more than 200 civilian UN international functionaries have died, and adhere anonymously to the standards of their service. A handful, from time to time, have yielded to corruption: in early 2004 charges of the diversion of great sums from the cancelled Oil for Food Programme for Iraq between the two wars there were being investigated.[15]

Preserving the international civil service

Although governments pledge to honor the international status of the United Nations, their own interpretations guide them in applying the law of the Charter against trying to influence the Secretariat as it performs its duties. Beyond the top-level "gentleman's agreement" and the widespreading practice of shopping for appointments, some UN members could be accused of ignoring their obligations to protect what are intended to be safeguards of impartiality. Their manipulations extend from the Secretary-General downwards to the lowest rungs of the international civil service. The Cold War produced celebrated examples, but others have since surfaced.

Pressure by the United States during the Cold War on the international civil service had an obvious origin in domestic politics. Urged on by some members of Congress and by the head of the Federal Bureau of Investigation, large sections of public opinion became convinced that the UN Secretariat was sheltering American nationals who favored Communism. President Truman eventually created a structure for advising the Secretary-General before appointments were made of candidates holding views objectionable to the United States. Some Americans serving on the UN staff were called before Congressional committees to testify about their political views and rumors of espionage; some of them declined to answer, in accordance with the Fifth Amendment of the US Constitution, and were subsequently discharged from the Secretariat.[16] For a time, the passports of American nationals in the Secretariat were not renewed. Secretary-General Lie permitted the FBI to enter the UN premises, presumably shielded by a formal agreement with United States from such intrusion, to contact members of the staff. At some political risk, Hammarskjöld promptly cancelled that permission.[17] But he and successors had to live with the American practice of vetting nominees for "loyalty" until 1986.

Under pressure of varying intensity but long duration from Congress, the US government has complained to the Secretary-General and the General Assembly of inefficiency and waste in the Secretariat. This has the effect of impeding appointments to the Secretariat, as well as blocking American contributions to the expenses of the organization. It also underlies the creation of an inspector-general's function at the top of the Secretariat.

When the People's Republic of China replaced the Taiwan-based regime in China's UN seat in 1971, the Beijing regime promptly demanded discharge of some Chinese members of the Secretariat. Similar incidents had occurred earlier when a Communist regime took power in Czechoslovakia. The Secretary-General usually found ways to avoid the dismissals. In these cases and others, the Secretary-General established some precedents that helped protect his authority and the integrity of the international service. At the same time, such incidents showed how member governments could threaten individual staff members.

Another practice that sows uncertainty appeared in Soviet-dominated Eastern Europe where UN staff members who were visiting on home leave were not allowed to return to their posts. Some few were held in jail. This, combined with refusal to allow Secretariat members to hold indefinite contracts rather than fixed-term appointments, frequently for only two or three years, helped to assure national control rather than international status.

For those who support the concept of an international civil service, it would be comforting to assume that the end of the Cold War had wiped away practices intended to influence Secretariat officials, but they still occur in the name of national interest, and not exclusively in former Soviet territory or in the United States.

Budget

The UN budget is prepared by the Secretariat and sent to the General Assembly by the Secretary-General. "The formulation of the budget ... is one of the most important tools at the disposal of the Secretary-General in leading, shaping, and coordinating the work of the organization", wrote Kofi Annan when he was the official in charge of putting it together.[18] It reflects not only all the activities of the organization but also a complex process by which member governments can follow the programs they approve and also try to block whatever they find objectionable. Increasingly the budget has nevertheless become a rudimentary but increasingly sharp tool of management, especially with the burgeoning use of information technology to link performance with expenditure.

As is the practice wherever a legislature makes the final budgetary review, the thick documents coming from the Secretary-General contain proposals for ultimate decision. However much they are based on the language emanating from the ECOSOC or the Security Council, the General Assembly has the final word on what actually is appropriated. The Secretary-General then either limps along on what is approved or serenely strides along on properly financed tracks.

The making of the UN budget comprises a labyrinthine process, promoted in large part by governments with highly organized bureaucracies and the wealth to pay large contributions. The poor countries usually show strong interest only in expanding the budget, especially where it touches on economic development, and less enthusiasm for the details of management. The cycle begins with the budget of the year before, the instructions to the Secretary-General from other organs about starting, ending or continuing programs, and an assortment of imperatives such as career contracts for employees, the maintenance of buildings and the proposals for the costs of the regional commissions. The UN budget covers two years – the second year rolls into the first year of the next biennium so that the General Assembly annually decides on a biennial budget.

Each department of the Secretariat puts together a budgetary request for the next biennium. This is passed along to the Department of Management, which has responsibility for drafting a document that the Secretary-General can present to the General Assembly for detailed debate in the Fifth (administrative and budgetary) Committee, and eventual passage. Ambitious and serious bureaucrats seek, of course, to improve their work, and the less zealous at least to protect their functions. Therefore, budget-making impels competition within the Secretariat. This is played out in a set of committees and discussions at each hierarchical level. It eventually leads to decisions by the Secretary-General on what he will support and what he will refuse. Thus, the budget aggregates important management and policy implications.

Within that process, however, the hot breath of the General Assembly, led by its relatively small group of dedicated managerial specialists, can soon be felt. Even before a good draft of some sections can be put together, the primary watchdog, the Advisory Committee on Administrative and Budgetary Questions (ACABQ) – which is manned by formally independent experts who happen, however, to be nominated by their governments – may be consulted on some items. Less formally, some governments may, early in the process, try to persuade the Secretariat that a proposed item either reflects miserliness or profligacy. Such claims have an obviously political, not technical, motivation.

Furthermore, two other watchdogs may breathe hard. From inside the Secretariat, the Office of International Oversight Services may have issued a report that affects either the process of budgeting or some existing program. The other, the Board of Auditors, is composed, like ACABQ, formally of independent experts but chosen because they are senior governmental auditors. Its reports could disclose deficiencies which would need remedies.

Even with a document that is officially approved by the Secretary-General, the process is far from over. The ACABQ examines it and issues a report to the General Assembly which practically always seeks to hold back spending and suggest marginal organizational improvements. At the same time, a 21-member intergovernmental Committee on Program and Coordination functions to restrain expensive development and humanitarian undertakings; in fact, it was organized in 1966 in the midst of one of the recurring financial crises as a means for the rich countries, led by the United States, to press to minimize the budget and, thus, their contributions. By consensus – which indicates a bargaining process – it submits very detailed comments on the budget proposed by the Secretary-General. All of this is set against a background decision by the General Assembly, which, despite an expanding agenda, has held the *real*, but not nominal, increase in the UN budget at zero from 1990 until 2003.

When the General Assembly takes up the budget proposed by the Secretary-General, it has a vast documentation that includes what is technically described as a performance budget, various analyses from its own nominally expert organs, and whatever the 191 government delegates to the Fifth Committee have in their briefcases. Among the expert organs that report is its own Joint Inspection Unit, headquartered in Geneva and comprising 11 inspectors, some of whom have had diplomatic careers. Its members act nominally in their personal capacity in investigating specific organizational topics approved by the Assembly.

In actuality, the budget process is costly and the real decision-making hard to follow. Only specialists can contribute significantly and, in fact, a relatively few governments can send really knowledgeable representatives to the General Assembly. Nor are some representatives helped by the fact that a colleague from his government in another committee has supported an expensive project while to the representative in the Fifth Committee the instruction is to hold down expenditure. That does not mean that the discussions have no meaning. It provides a last chance to exercise a financial veto on a policy or to inject an unplanned bonus. How seriously they are taken can be seen in the troubled mien of the Secretariat officials, their efforts to defend or clarify the documents, and their willingness to try to meet the demands of committee members. All concerned, however little or much expertness they have, know that their concurrence or opposition will shape the work of the Secretariat in the years ahead.

Growth of UN budget

Regular Annual UN Budget listed by decennia:

1946	US$19 million
1956	US$49 million
1966	US$122 million
1976	US$373 million
1986	US$856 million
2003	US$1,000 million (approximately)

Source: UN budget documents submitted to General Assembly

All of this effort works out a bill of slightly in excess of US$1 billion per year for what is called the regular budget. To give some idea of the magnitude of this outlay, it is less than 10 percent of the annual budget of the United States Department of State and about 11 percent more than the operating budget of Princeton University. Aside from the strictly central UN share of the budget, a supplementary tally is added for the expenses of military missions for peace maintenance, some of which is usually assumed by the donor countries. This component often adds an amount of roughly the same magnitude as the regular budget, although it varies with the missions and other projects that are approved. In 2002/3, biennial estimates for field missions and other activities and funds aside from the regular budget came to US$7,260 million. Some of the extrabudgetary (as the UN jargon designates them) expenses include the costs of such items as the special International Tribunals for War Crimes in Yugoslavia and in Rwanda and provisions for contingencies and emergencies. In addition, a separate account has been created for major maintenance and enlargement of the UN Headquarters in New York, which was built for a membership list of around 100. Once approved by the General Assembly, the budget then signifies the appropriation to payment for salaries of UN functionaries, other expenses associated with running the organization, including its regional commissions and offices, and the expenses of the International Court of Justice, plus the costs of the field missions for peace.

Budgets for UNDP, UNICEF, the UN Population Fund and UNHCR get a separate treatment from their own directing boards. What they determine appears in overall documents but is subject to a somewhat different process and should be regarded as a formal but not actual addition to the bill for the central Secretariat.

Finance

Although finance – that is, providing money to pay the bills and salaries – is strictly speaking much less a matter for the Secretary-General than for governments among themselves, it conditions everything that the Secretariat does. Contributing to the UN treasury to pay for the organizational budget, as decided by the General Assembly, is a legal obligation for every member, according to the UN Charter which has been reinforced by judicial interpretation by the International Court of Justice.[19] In terse wording, Article 17 of the Charter provides that "[t]he expenses of the Organization be borne by the Members as apportioned by the General Assembly". In essence, that provision opens a door for going beyond what is to be paid and turns concentration on who pays. Moreover, Article 19 of the Charter offers the possibility of suspending the governments that fall more than two years behind in contributions from voting in the General Assembly; this provision is rarely invoked and always causes a storm when it is threatened.

The Secretariat's role in this arena is mainly technical although Secretaries-General have more than once voiced a mournful opinion about the justice of what emerges. Moreover, as the United States fell behind in its obligatory contributions, especially for peace-maintenance expenses, as the twentieth century was ending, the Secretary-General frequently had to plead with governments to pay up.[20] During Boutros-Ghali's term, the arrears reached the point where the Secretary-General had to declare publicly that, if more cash did not come in within a month, the organization would be unable to pay the salaries of the Secretariat.

The stance of the United States, dictated in the American budgeting process in the Congress,[21] both underlay the cash crisis and imposed political conditions on paying up arrears. By 1999, Washington owed US$167.9 million, or more than two-thirds of the total arrears list for the central UN budget. Moreover, it was US$53 million behind in its payments for peace-maintaining missions and owed another US$7.2 million for the war crimes tribunals. Thus, the biggest single contributor – and, as the developing country governments tirelessly pointed out, the richest country in the world – was able by itself to threaten all UN work.

What each government is obliged to contribute to the UN budget is set out in a scale of assessments. This is recommended to the General Assembly by the intergovernmental 18-member Committee on Contributions. The innocent-sounding title masks a good deal of pressure and dealing in relation to the crucial methodology of the scale of assessments. In essence, this takes into account the economic ability of a government to pay and the population of a member, although a limit is set on the maximum proportion of the budget that any one country can pay. This has long been a crucial issue for the United States government, driven by Congressional criticism. The United States began by paying 40 percent and then 33 percent of the contributions; this was reduced by the General Assembly to 25 percent as more members were added and some became richer. Under enormous pressure from the US Congress in the late 1990s, which systematically withheld large parts of the contribution the government owed, it was reduced again to 22 percent. This does not yet satisfy Congressional critics. The least developed, small countries receive bills for only 0.001 percent of the total. Some two-thirds of the financing comes from the seven most industrialized countries. A somewhat different, agreed scale is used for peace-making or peace-enforcing mission which obliges the permanent members of the Security Council to pay a greater proportion of the total. The rest are spread out at various levels with the governments of wealthy countries paying more and the least developed only nominal amounts.

Management, finances and national politics

The significance of technical approaches to management of the Secretariat can only be understood from a broad perspective that is colored by both national and international political relationships. Concepts such as efficiency and economy of operations collide quickly with policies and demands from capitals and the prestige that national delegations to the UN maintain as evidence of sovereignty.

Nowhere has this been more evident than in the financial arena. The UN core and the associated agencies established by the General Assembly depend on contributions from member governments. In the case of the regular UN budget these are legal obligations; in the case of the other agencies, such as UNHCR, and some extrabudgetary items, governments contribute what they wish. In any case, in the end taxpayers are directed by governments to reach into their pockets for resources. The financial issue thus may become one of national politics.

Withholding of contributions as a means of objecting to a UN activity began early on. The Soviet Union and its allies, for instance, declined to pay for the costs of maintaining the UN Cemetery in Korea that contains the graves of soldiers of several countries which had sent troops to repel the invasion by North Korea in 1950. Moscow claimed that as the mandate delivered by the Security Council that set up the force was illegal so were all expenses attached to it. France joined the list of withholders after the creation by the General Assembly of the UN Emergency Force during the Suez conflict in 1956 (see Chapter 4). Both France, which had joined the United Kingdom in the attack on Egypt, and the Soviet Union declined to pay their assigned share of the bills. This eventually led to the Soviet Union's arrears being so great that the United States originated an abortive attempt to apply Article 19 in order to embarrass Moscow by depriving it of its voice in the General Assembly. That led to the advisory opinion of the International Court of Justice that the regular budget approved by the General Assembly was a legal obligation on

UN members. The decision was largely drafted by Philip Jessup, the American judge on the tribunal.

Thirty years later it was the United States that held the leading position for budget arrears. As Congress steadily declined fully to honor the requests by the President to pay up the contribution, the arrears, augmented by increasing peace-keeping operations, only mounted. The financial crises, especially during Boutros-Ghali's tenure, opened an opportunity for members of Congress, led by the Republican Senator Jesse Helms who was chairman of the foreign relations committee, to decry UN efficiency and alleged UN threats to national sovereignty. Only after much strife, the veto of a second term for Boutros-Ghali, and prolonged negotiation that included an appearance by Helms in the Security Council, was Annan able to reach some accommodation. The negotiations were critically augmented with a US$45 million gift from the American entrepreneur, Ted Turner, who also established the private United Nations Foundation to assist UN projects.[22] In the aftermath of the terrorist attacks on the United States in 2002, the Congress promptly appropriated money, largely to pay up the debt that the Secretary-General billed, and thus no doubt hoping to assure multinational cooperation against terrorism – itself an old but not heretofore exciting UN agenda item.

Meantime, the United States Government repeatedly put pressure on the Secretary-General and his staff to increase efficiency, accountability and cost-cutting. This, in part, would satisfy Congress. It would also gain favor from the governments that, like Washington, wanted to keep their contributions as low as they could. So micro-management of the UN Secretariat became a tool for some Congressmen to develop criticism of the relationship between the United States and the UN and as a means for opposing UN policies.

The effects of the barrage of criticism had some positive but still insufficient consequences for management.[23] The gradual creation of rational budgetary tools that made clearer what the UN Secretariat did and what it accomplished was one outcome. Arguably, another was the creation of an inspector-general's office in the Secretariat. These measures not only shed more light on what the UN did and did not do, but also equipped with some tools of modern public management an office that was largely created in a diplomatic image. Incidentally, it also stimulated modernization of the information technology available to the UN (see Chapter 6). Beyond that, it demonstrated once more that global activities were driven by complex relationships between national politics, international organizations, and diplomatic patchwork.

4 The Secretary-General as world constable

The Secretary-General's relationship to the work of the Security Council gives him an aura of the world's constable. It resembles the model of the classical British "bobby", the police officer who, backed by law and without weapons more threatening than a baton, patrols dangerous streets to offer help and protection to the public. The metaphor accurately suggests that the Secretary-General can collect information and draw conclusions about threats to international peace and security. His signals of trouble ahead serve as his baton. In some circumstances, he may intervene in quarrels to create a mood, or even a process, to further conciliation. These gestures, even when backed by responses from persuasive governments, may not succeed. And like a classical constable, the Secretary-General cannot pronounce binding judgments as to guilt or innocence, or apply punishment. Rather, he can sometimes start a process of judgment and eventual enforcement.

All of this is stated or implied in Article 99 of the UN Charter that authorizes the Secretary-General to bring before the Security Council anything that in his opinion may threaten or breach the peace. As the Secretary-General heads a principal UN organ and sits with the representatives of the 15 governments that make up the Security Council, he is at least guaranteed access to its formal deliberations.

This chapter takes up the role of the Secretary-General in what the UN Charter and broad opinion set out as the primary function of the organization – that is, maintaining peace and security. It treats the means available to the Secretary-General and the constraints on his developing policies and carrying them out. It examines his activities in several UN responses to active and possible threats to the peace.

Inherent opportunities and limitations

Closely inspected, the analogy of the constable differs from the actuality of the Secretary-General's position. Unlike the constable, he participates or sometimes even leads the way in making policy to prevent disturbances to the peace. His role ultimately is political in intent and implication, and differs fundamentally from merely carrying out orders and duties passed down by political authority. Although the Secretary-General can call a matter of peace and security to the attention of the Security Council, it does not, however, automatically – or sometimes even show inclination to – follow his lead. Its members set the agenda, on occasion decline even to examine the opinion of the Secretary-General, and usually hesitate to apply coercion to offenders. Taking his cue from the reticence of the Council to act as enforcer, the Secretary-General rarely has explicitly used Article 99 as it may generate division in the Security Council around the ultimate obligation to apply force. Beyond a formal warning of trouble, he can deliver information and, moreover, discuss possible or actual threats to the peace in public speeches. He can offer analysis in his *Annual Report on the Work of the Organization* and other documents as possible contributions to long-term recommendations by the General Assembly.

As the Security Council primarily deals with immediate challenges rather than long-term programs, what the Secretary-General brings to it usually relates to the current news, to operations in progress, to anticipation of danger, and the like. Some of his information, which is a principal and crucial component of any approach to the Security Council, comes from the continuing conversations that he and his senior officials have with the representatives of governments and often their chiefs.[1] This doubtless provides a basis for understanding tension among governments and to some extent of internal strife, such as insurrections or large-scale violations of human rights, that may have transnational effects and thus eventually engage the Security Council. Garnering information follows the canon of classical diplomacy that emphasizes knowing what is going on. It helps the Secretary-General to judge what would be acceptable to the Council and to the parties to a dispute. Hammarskjöld described the network that the Secretary-General could tap as a ceaseless diplomatic conference.[2]

Some of the information that reaches the Secretary-General through the diplomatic network reflects the work of clandestine intelligence services operated mainly by the larger governments. As he has it second-hand, it must be handled gingerly, for its sources may remain obscure and the tenor of such informal transmissions is frequently tuned to support the government that hands it over. The Secretariat often, perhaps usually, has little notion of what is omitted. Its effect on the conclusions drawn by the Secretary-General and his staff seems beyond generalization except in instances that leave little doubt, such as photographs taken by both commercial and military surveillance satellites.

The Secretary-General's own staff comprises an internal source of information that may be more systematic and comprehensive than diplomatic whispers. The Secretariat has always included a political affairs department as well as specialists in the Secretary-General's immediate office. They collect data, no doubt most of it from public sources, analyze it and present conclusions and recommendations to the Secretary-General through formal bureaucratic channels and via its senior specialists in discussions with their peers. The internal papers – the analytical reports passed to colleagues and superiors in the bureaucracy – estimate the dimensions and gravity of developments affecting peace and security, and form an integral, but varying, part of the decisional process that underlies what the Secretary-General tells the Security Council. Concerned mainly with policy, the political affairs department, despite the magnitude of its field of surveillance, is small, especially in comparison with the vast bureaus of London, Paris, Tokyo or Beijing.[3] The legal office of the Secretariat also advises on the relevant international law.[4]

Other informational sources feed with a variety of enthusiasm and expertness into the decisional process. The UN Development Program stations its country chiefs, a good many of whom have diplomatic experience, in more than 100 countries. Following ideas supported by the Secretary-General and endorsed by governments, the UNDP representatives function in capitals as directors of a UN house and thus as nominal coordinator of all programs mounted by the several autonomous agencies of the UN system. This structure has occasionally been a useful source of information, especially in local crises. The Department of Public Information has maintained 70 information offices scattered around the world (see Chapter 6). These report on what the mass media distributes in their regions and keep contact with NGOs as well as furnishing information and answering questions about the UN. In some instances, its directors, by interpreting what is featured in the mass media and what their contacts have to say, can assist in political analysis. The salience of these sources depends on the talents of the field personnel and the efficiency of internal coordination within the Secretariat, and thus raises eternal issues of management in a large public agency.

A long list of field missions approved by the Security Council more directly connects with on-going violence. Some date back to the Israeli–Arab armistice of 1948 and the equally old conflict between India and Pakistan over who rules Kashmir. Here peacekeeping soldiers, observers or other watch-dog arrangements, under direction of the Secretary-General and his Department of Peacekeeping Operations, provide direct but hardly exclusive lines to trouble spots. Their continuing flow of reports may furnish additional information for analysis of known conflicts and the basis for proposing expansion of tasks.

Some of the reporting has an especially poignant character, as in the Rwanda genocide,[5] and on the slaughter of Muslim men at Srebrenica.[6] Even enterprising and eloquent reports, however, may fail to prepare either the Security Council or the Secretary-General for the breadth of

---

List of peace-keeping operations as of 2004

UN Truce Supervision Organization (1948) on Israel/Palestine borders

UN Military Observer Group in India and Pakistan (1949) in Kashmir

UN Peacekeeping Force in Cyprus (1964)

UN Disengagement Observer Force (1974) on Golan Heights, Israel/Syria/Lebanon

UN Interim Force in Lebanon (1978) in south Lebanon

MINURSO (UN Mission for the Referendum in Western Sahara) (1991) in Mauritania/Morocco

UN Observer Mission in Georgia (1993)

UN Interim Administration Mission in Kosovo (1993)

UN Mission in Sierra Leone (1999)

MONUC (UN Organization Mission in the Democratic Republic of the Congo (1999) in eastern Congo

UN Mission in Ethiopia and Eritrea (2000)

UN Mission of Support in East Timor (2002)

UN Mission in Liberia (2003)

UN Operation in Ivory Coast (2004)

MINUSTAH (UN Stabilization Mission in Haiti) (2004)

ONUB (UN Operation in Burundi) (2004)

Source: United Nations, www.un.org/Depts/dpko/dpko.bnote.htm

an on-coming disaster. Nor, as in the Rwanda case – about which Annan, who had headed the peacekeeping department, acknowledged failure and "deep remorse"[7] – does the Secretariat always fully appreciate the significance of the reports.

Putting the informational and diplomatic resources together into a digested pattern that can form the basis for a political function of the Secretary-General, which is itself not beyond controversy, remains a constant puzzle. Some progress has been made in setting up an early-warning office that is equipped with new technical analytical devices. After the faltering of a limited Office of Research and Collection of Information, Boutros-Ghali abolished it. Anticipating crises derives some support from other parts of the UN system, such as the Food and Agriculture Organization (FAO) and UNHCR that assemble data which can forecast famine and movement of people. But the United Nations does not have access to the extensive satellite observation systems and listening facilities of the most powerful governments, such as the United States, Russia, France, and China, unless exceptionally they offer it or are successfully petitioned for it. Expensive commercial satellite services also can on occasion be tapped.

Nor does the Secretary-General have anything like a standing diplomatic service that keeps trouble spots under constant surveillance. Every attempt, indeed, to develop such a service or something resembling it so far has simply stimulated resentment and opposition from the partisans of unencumbered national sovereignty and from governments that fear close observation. As a partial substitute, the Secretaries-General have used the device of personal representatives, who undertake informational or conciliation missions to the sites of political disturbance.[8] These have often ended with little result beyond information, as has been the case with representatives seeking to ameliorate the conflicts around Israel or the mission abandoned in 2004 by former US Secretary of State James Baker to find a way out of the decades-long strife surrounding the Western Sahara now occupied by Morocco. Some other representatives are appointed with a watching brief on a troubling situation, such as the human rights representative, a Malaysian diplomat, for Myanmar or the former foreign minister of Canada for the dispute between Eritrea and Ethiopia.

In another instance, the negotiations conducted by Lakhdar Brahimi, a former Algerian foreign minister, as a special representative of the Secretary-General to Iraq in 2004, had far-reaching results.[9] It led to a deep revision of the American plan for developing a constitution and the appointment of a government to claim sovereignty, write a constitution, and hold elections. This was all the more noteworthy as

Annan earlier had in his usual calm way expressed open skepticism about the US-led armed effort in 2003, without a specific Security Council directive, to depose Saddam Hussein, the Iraqi head of state

As many field missions approved by the Security Council employ military personnel, the Secretary-General requires appropriate specialized advice. For much of the existence of the United Nations, the military engaged in various missions were not even accurately tracked in a 24-hour, seven-day situation room. That has changed and now a small military advisory staff keeps watch and advises the Secretary-General and colleagues in the political affairs and peacekeeping operations departments.

The standard operation of the Secretariat does on occasion result in headlines about humanitarian disasters that have security implication. In 2004, for instance, field missions began to report on growing misery and destruction in the western province of Darfur in Sudan. The Under-Secretary-General for Humanitarian Affairs appeared in the Security Council to describe a growing crisis that included "ethnic cleansing",[10] a descriptive phrase for deadly programs employed by the combatants in Bosnia-Herzegovina. Although the first response was limited to a call by the Council to the parties to reach a cease-fire and protect civilians, it meant at least that governments could not plead ignorance of the facts. By late 2004, the Security Council had adopted resolutions that intimated coercive action and asked the Secretary-General to set up an independent group to determine if genocide had occurred. Yet the number of affected persons reached estimates of more than 1,500,000 by the autumn of 2004 and Jan Pronk, the special representative of the Secretary-General, told the Council that the Sudan government had done nothing effective to stop insecurity.

In a few instances, the Secretary-General himself has undertaken such a mission, as Waldheim did, with a nearly fatal outcome, during the crisis caused by the hostage-taking of American diplomats in Iran in 1979.[11] Annan optimistically undertook a similar effort in 2000 to Baghdad that ended without bringing the government of Saddam Hussein to conform with the orders of the Security Council. Annan timed a visit to Khartoum, the Sudanese capital, to complement a similar appearance of the American Secretary of State as the Darfur crisis intensified in 2004. The earlier mission by Hammarskjöld to free the American airmen held in China had established a precedent for such visits.[12]

In fact, the Secretary-General relies for the most part on time-honored diplomatic methods in deciding whether the Security Council should be told of a threat or breach of the peace. This includes a dose of intuitive appreciation of what is known and what is likely to be accepted by governments. If these methods were to lead the Secretary-General into hasty or unwarranted conclusions, the importance of the office would suffer. Furthermore, an impolitic gesture can produce the kind of acute reverse pressure that has been notoriously exerted by the Soviet Union and the United States on the Secretary-General personally and his office generally.

The end of the Cold War both simplified and complicated the concerns of the Secretary-General in maintaining peace and security. No longer was there automatic tension between the two leading powers in the Security Council. But neither was there anything like full agreement between the United States and the other veto-bearers. What was once a fairly clear line-up of those governments that favored one or other of the Cold Warriors, or tried to steer clear of both of them, quickly evaporated. In its place came less predictable positions, both in the Security Council and outside it, and more emphasis on national aims. Moreover, new causes of concern, such as failed states and internal conflicts with widespread regional effects, engaged the Council as they had not in the earlier times of a bi-polar world. The Security Council, along with the Secretary-General and the Secretariat, were busier than ever.

Nevertheless, the use of coercion to enforce the decisions of the Security Council and its aftermath probably would almost always nurse at least some controversy among the broader UN membership, much of which regards sovereignty as the paramount guide to policy. Consequently, most of the time, the Secretary-General estimates that restraint in using his formal political role in the Security Council, and Article 99 in particular, produces better results than frequent, however merited, dramatic gestures.

Enforcement action

In contrast to the apocalyptic delusions of some right-wing vigilante movements in the United States of the 1990s, the Secretariat has no arms at its disposal. The Secretary-General cannot order even one helicopter, black or otherwise, into battle. His responsibility for directing a few, mainly small, military elements that generally engage in no battles has usually taken form under decisions of the Security Council based on Chapter VI of the UN Charter. It provides for pacific settlement of disputes. It contrasts with Chapter VII of the Charter where provisions for a military force under the command of the Permanent Members are set out. In fact, the antagonisms of the

Cold War aborted that notion which is now only the ghost of never-executed planning. That has not prevented the Security Council from approving a rare enforcement mission, incorporating armed units contributed by several countries. These have seldom been put under the overall supervision of the Secretary-General or used the Secretariat as a chain of command.

Two major examples of large-scale enforcement missions in inter-state conflicts illustrate the distance of the Secretary-General from the actual command structures in large actions. The first of these dates back to 1950, when the Security Council ordered a response to the North Korean invasion of the Republic of Korea in the south of the peninsula. This quick decision became possible because of a coincidence: the Soviet Union, which later angrily protested what had been done, had absented its representative in protest against the presence of the Kuomintang delegate, rather than that of the Communist regime in Beijing. The concern of the United Nations in Korea, divided because of the Cold War, had begun three years before with an attempt by the General Assembly, led by the United States, to bring about unification of the peninsula and to organize elections. The attack from the North exploded while a UN commission with observational and electoral responsibilities was in place.[13]

In the wake of the 1950 attack, the Security Council appointed the United States government as its military agent. A large air, ground and naval force led by Washington eventually included 16 other governments as well as the Republic of Korea. Reports on this campaign came through military channels via the United States government to the Security Council. The United States, rather than the Security Council, accepted a ceasefire and led the still unsuccessful armistice negotiations with North Korea under the UN flag. From then on, outside the UN structure, the United States assisted the Republic of Korea in reconstruction, kept a major force there to ward off a new attack and left no useful room for UN decisions. Secretary-General Lie, who had supported the action of the Security Council, had little role there, even though he had tried without result to convince the United States that his Secretariat ought to be brought closer to the political direction.[14] The peninsula still divided, the two Koreas eventually became UN members.

The second major improvised enforcement action was mandated by the Security Council in resolution S/660 of 2 August 1990 immediately after the attack by Iraq on Kuwait. This onslaught unquestionably violated the UN Charter. By then, the Cold War no longer dominated UN proceedings. An armed response, built up under American leadership over many months, proceeded with approval not only from Security Council members but also from a majority of neighboring countries in the Middle East.

Beyond the region, most other governments supported an armed response that was systematically organized by the United States, much as had been the outcome in haste during the more controversial action in Korea. The resulting sub-contracted force included 28 allies that contributed troops. It first expelled the Iraqi force from Kuwait in January 1991 and by the end of February conquered what was left of the invaders in a few hours.

The United States government in fact directed the war and made the decision to halt its attack at the gates of Baghdad. The government of Saddam Hussein remained in place and only part of Iraq fell under the command of the UN-mandated force which soon withdrew the ground elements and left a small air and naval force in place. The Security Council directed the Secretary-General to take on numerous tasks that involved humanitarian programs, legal remedies for damage and preventive observation on the southern border.

The two major enforcement cases made clear that the command would be placed by the Security Council in the available hands of a leading military power. It could sub-contract part of the action to voluntary partners. The Secretary-General would then have a marginal supporting role. This organizational approach differs, however, from the "coalition of the willing" organized by the United States for the second conflict with Iran as the Security Council did not adopt a specific authorization.

Basic peacekeeping

A product of political imagination and a dangerous episode of the Cold War, the model of basic peacekeeping was first employed in the Suez crisis of 1956, at the same moment that the Soviet Union sent tanks into Hungary to suppress dissension in its bloc. Basic peace-keeping still serves as a conceptual base line.[15] It was devised largely by Hammarskjöld, and his immediate staff, and Lester Pearson, the Canadian statesman, as a means of separating Israeli, British and French attackers from the Egyptian defenders of the Suez Canal. It also made possible for the Secretariat to organize the clearing of the blocked waterway.[16] Nothing specific in the UN Charter provided a legal basis for peacekeeping, which Hammarskjöld famously described as "Chapter Six-and-One-Half", that is between pacific settlement of disputes in Chapter VI and enforcement in Chapter VII.

The essence of basic peacekeeping drew on earlier UN experience in using military observers in Kashmir and Palestine.[17] It relies on an armistice for fighting forces and their governments' invitation to the United Nations. To observation, it adds specific provisions for stationing troops between the parties to encourage compliance with the armistice. The UN troops carry only light arms, which they may use only in self-defense and not for coercion. The troop contributors would not include the Permanent Five of the Security Council. The Secretary-General and his staff supervise the deployment and activity. This device in the Suez Crisis came to be called the UN Emergency Force (UNEF).

The field intelligence transmitted to New York came directly from a UN-appointed commander who had been serving as head of an existing observation mission in the Israeli border area. UNEF operated in the Suez area until the outbreak of the 1967 war between Israel and its Arab neighbors. In a controversial decision, it was withdrawn then by U Thant who asserted that it no longer had support from the troop contributors.[18]

Before then, Hammarskjöld had used the model, this time with Security Council authority, to respond to the breakdown of order and government in the newly independent Congo in 1960. The conflict, however, did not cross international borders and involved barely disciplined fighting units, but it attracted a great deal of manipulation in the background by the Soviet Union and the United States. Despite the intense political pressure on both Hammarskjöld and then Thant, the barely appropriate model was adapted to preserve the Congo against secessionist tendencies.[19] But to do so, force was used in a manner that seemingly violated the basic peacekeeping model. It also strained, sometimes to a breaking point, the ability of the Secretary-General and the Secretariat to supervise the ground level actions.

Nevertheless, during the Cold War neither the Security Council nor the Secretary-General abandoned peacekeeping as useful in defined circumstances. For example, peacekeeping forces were in place in 2004 in the Golan Heights, in the corner where Israel, Lebanon and Syria abut, and in Cyprus. The conditions matched those required by classical peacekeeping.

Expanded peacekeeping

An unanticipated result of some UN peacekeeping ventures, as in the Congo, led to sizable governing effort under the direction of the Secretary-General. Such activity constituted perhaps an even greater novelty for an international organization than were the techniques of basic peacekeeping. Over time, it often appeared, governing ventures can stimulate opposition on the ground and little popularity among the UN members, especially those that hold any hint of dilution of national authority.

Nevertheless, demands for peacekeeping, dubbed "second generation,"[20] that expanded to creation or propping up of state institutions have added heavy responsibilities for the Secretary-General and staff.[21] While such efforts do not always include specific programs of military force, heavier armaments often come along with the contributed soldiers.

Although each case of expanded peacekeeping has had its particularities, all have comprised extensive assistance to the host state. This has included furnishing normal state services as well as receiving material assistance from abroad. One of the most elaborate of the missions dispatched by the Security Council operated in Cambodia in the three years beginning in 1991.[22] It involved the insertion of 22,000 peacekeepers and civilian personnel, who were instructed to hold elections and establish a government to succeed the genocidal regime of Pol Pot. Headed by Yasushi Akashi of Japan as special representative of the Secretary-General, the mission included not only pacification, agreed upon by the several local contenders for power, but also in effect a temporary government. The election was indeed held to general satisfaction of outside observers, a government was organized, and the military elements and most of the rest of the UN mission were withdrawn. Parts of the UN system stayed on to help the new government with reconstruction and development. A decade later it was apparent that UN-guided procedures to build a government had hardly healed the scars of the past nor installed a fleckless democracy. At the same time, though, the level of violence had been greatly reduced and a functioning government was in place.

These two incidents made clear that expanded peacekeeping involved difficult decisions. Some conceptual contradiction between the pacific settlement model and enforcement demanded adaptation. Furthermore, continuing support under difficult circumstances from principal donors of financing and troops was sometimes unavailable. These difficulties sharpened the point that engagement of the UN mechanism did not necessarily lead to desired conclusions if local groups declined to cooperate or use their own weapons to brush aside demands from New York and from lightly armed UN forces on the ground. They put obvious strains on the office of the Secretary-General and the broader staff that lacked standing organization to cope with such broad challenges.[23]

Despite the challenges, however, openings in the Cold War fabric provided enough to mount UN peacekeeping missions in Afghanistan, Central America, and Namibia and Angola. Each had some attributes of the two largest second-generation efforts and none fitted the classical model.

Peacekeeping with enforcement

The presumed sharp line between pacific settlements of disputes, set out in Chapter VI of the UN Charter, and the coercive measures that the Security Council could organize under Chapter VII, blurred with the stretching of the peacekeeping concept. Looking towards a higher chapter number, however, did anything but guarantee commensurate political and military commitment of the UN members.

The use of UN forces to defeat secessionist elements in the Congo by aerial bombardment and heavy ground units strongly suggested that without all of the conditions of the basic peacekeeping model in place, the original concept could hardly be successfully applied. If no large-scale force was used by UN troops in Cambodia, some strenuous local military engagements took place. In Somalia, the mission ended with a small-scale fight, not authorized by the UN command on the ground, and some futile engagements of UN peacekeepers who expected a different mode of action. In all of these examples, the Secretary-General and his staff were hard put to provide adequate guidance to the commanders. Nor could the Security Council be relied upon to adapt its instructions to local developments.

Whatever the legal and practical obscurities that condition UN responses to fighting and human destruction, novel combinations of peacekeeping and military force were undertaken in the last years of the twentieth century and at the beginning of the twenty-first. As with the earlier situations in the Congo and Cambodia, the new conflicts did not grow out of classical international war but rather collapsing local authority, insurrections and ethnic animosities. They created large-scale human suffering.

The most complex of these UN operations had its roots in the dissolution of Yugoslavia in the last decade of the twentieth century.[24] From outside the country, the political responses, in which units of the Secretariat were directly engaged, focused at first on fears of wide civil warfare and of conflicts among the component republics of Yugoslavia. Eventually, attention in the Security Council centered on Bosnia-Herzegovina where fighting organized around the Serbian, Muslim and Croatian ethnic groups in the country, along with support from outside the province, was destroying cities, emptying the countryside, and filling cemeteries and brutal prison camps. The Security Council had earlier dispatched peacekeepers under the classical formula but had been promised the assistance, if requested by the Secretary-General, from aircraft under the command of the North Atlantic Treaty Organization (NATO). The Security Council also designated some towns as safe zones without specifically defining what was meant.

If anything demonstrated the fragility of lightly armed peacekeepers in situations where the belligerents would not adhere to ceasefires, it was the disaster of Srebrenica, a small city that had once had a peaceful population, partly Serbian and partly Muslim, and was designated to be a safe zone. A small contingent of Dutch peacekeepers found itself increasingly restricted by ethnic-Serbian troops. Eventually the Dutch unit lost mobility. Its commander sought air support, which was declined in a chain of command that eventuated in the Secretary-General's office. Akashi was the senior UN representative in the field. He advised against air strikes, fearing attacks on the vulnerable peacekeepers elsewhere. He had concurring advice from the French general who headed the military command. The Serbs used the situation to separate several thousand Muslim men from the rest of the population. In what was seen as the worst example of genocidal behavior since the end of World War II, the Serbs were killed in the name of ethnic cleansing.[25] Only later was extra UN force and political pressure employed to bring some stability to the situation.

The background of the expanded peacekeeping mission in Somalia in 1992–1993 included some elements resembling those of Cambodia. Repression and denial of human rights and the failure of the government to provide security or services had led to unrest and violence among clan-based groups and the disappearance of the central authority. Like Cambodia, the evaporation of governance loaded heavy suffering on endemic poverty. Widespread concern among humanitarian organizations and graphic news reporting encouraged attention in member states and eventually in the Security Council. The UN already had a presence there in the shape of a force authorized to protect the delivery of relief supplies primarily through the International Committee of the Red Cross and with the fragile concurrence of leaders of clans. The United States took the lead in 1992 in the waning days of the presidency of George H.W. Bush to expand this minor force into a fully-fledged enforcement that would give more safety to the supply chain. It offered 22,000 troops, added to which another 10,000 came from 22 other governments. The

Security Council authorization left the command and control entirely in the hands of the United States and the Secretary-General with a watching brief.

That marginality of the Secretary-General changed sharply in a second phase of the operation. After the Clinton government took office in the United States, the Security Council decided to place the Secretary-General in charge of enforcement intended to end the interference of Somali warlords with relief efforts. Some 20,000 campaign-ready troops and nearly one-third that many logistical elements from a total of 33 countries were eventually deployed. An American military tint colored the operation as Boutros-Ghali appointed an American admiral as his personal representative and American warships lay over the horizon. The entire mission blew up, however, when a unit of US Rangers, intended as a rapid response force, was ordered into action independently of the UN command chain. Its target, a local warlord, inflicted heavy punishment on the unit and horrifying pictures of a dead American soldier being dragged through the streets of Mogadishu flared on television screens. The Clinton government decided no longer to support the Security Council decision, recalled its military and allowed the focus of blame to come onto Boutros-Ghali and the UN. The last of the UN force withdrew in 1995; nine years later there still was no functioning national government there.

In one part of the Yugoslav implosion, that of the turbulent Kosovo province where repression by Serbs had festered into rebellion by the Albanian majority, the United Nations was handed the job of actually managing the government so as to reconcile the ethnic groups. This long-term task included the stationing of NATO military units in the territory; should violence break out, as it did early in 2004, reinforcements could be sent by the NATO force stationed nearby in Bosnia-Herzegovina. It thus represented a rare instance in which the Secretariat worked with a military alliance not under the direction of the Security Council.

Broken states and human needs

UN responses to the collapse of states into civil war or lawlessness differ sharply from the presumption that international peace was characterized by the absence of attacks by one state on another. Yet almost universal opinion accepted that such situations deserve global action, usually by the United Nations. It was often formulated as "humanitarian intervention", a concept that attracted controversy and promotion of the idea that a "right to protect" should bind state policy.[26]

Such cases as the genocide in Cambodia, the collapse of Sierra Leone into violence, and similar implosions in Liberia and Somalia, as well as a few others of lesser magnitude, involve the UN in emergency relief to save populations from hunger, disease and homelessness. This precedes the revival or creation of new political and legal infrastructure as well as the use of military units. Often, as in Cambodia, the aim includes the building of orderly conditions to permit the election of a government. [27] In other instances, UN officials formally arrive to help the local officials but, in fact, as in the Congo during the 1960s and in Kosovo, they direct governance until tranquil relations develop between the contending local groups.

Such functions engage the Secretary-General and his staff in the delicate processes of reducing ethnic violence, usually with the help of peacekeeping troops with restricted mandates, demobilizing fighters and reviving governing processes and respect for human rights. Furthermore, as one informed observer remarks, "[i]n the absence of clear rules governing their conduct, international officials find themselves endowed with more or less absolute power".[28]

The UN itself obviously has insufficient staff, budget, or all the needed expertness to take on such ventures from top to bottom. Rather, the Secretariat and its chief have to give them some structure, solicit the financing, find the needed experts, set up field offices and provide the staff for them. To begin with, such missions involve the Secretary-General and his senior officers in consultations about the mandate to be adopted by the Security Council or the General Assembly. These diplomatic functions depend on the information and analysis that the Secretary-General can use, as well as on the parallel input from governments.

Once the mandate is in place, the Secretary-General has the task of leading the way to the actual creation of the field mission. This is usually preceded, as in some cases is the mandate, by an exploratory mission sent to the trouble spot to estimate the needs. The phase of assembling commitments to furnish even a modest number of military personnel, their movement to the field, and their continuing supply, may consume weeks, or more likely many months. Each step requires negotiations with donor government and with host authorities. Permanent staff has to be augmented with temporary help, some of which has sometimes been borrowed from governments. And each step can find the Secretary-General bruising delicate national toes. Once deployed, such a mission still has to tread warily. For example, the UN administration in Kosovo, writes a former UN official there, "has been forced to constantly reinvent and redefine its role and objections … by substituting the absence of a clear end state with a number of successive milestones".[29]

The needs of such broadened peacekeeping missions invariably include improvised humanitarian relief that may become large-scale. Implicitly, and sometimes explicitly, they tend to challenge the sole authority of the national government that the concept of sovereignty incorporates. Yet if a government cannot shape local conditions either to maintain security or to feed and house its nationals, other governments may expect a UN peacekeeping mission to fill the needs of human society.

Indeed one of the driving impulses for involving the United Nations can be found in camps for displaced populations and in medical needs, undernourishment, lack of employment and social disintegration. Modern mass communications spread poignant images of suffering and contribute to the acceptance of the United Nations as a device to bring succor. Specifically, the Secretariat now includes an Office for Coordination of Humanitarian Affairs which keeps watch on growing emergencies and is prepared to coordinate the efforts in the entire system of UN organizations to provide the needed help, including soliciting governments for financing and contributions-in-kind.

As the United Nations serves as one of the important central locations for dealing with humanitarian disasters, its staff members have not only experience with the needs but also direct relationships with help providers. Moreover, the organizational experience, personnel, and some substantial preparations for field operations exist in the associated international organizations of the UN system. Within the remit of the General Assembly is the UN High Commissioner for Refugees whose central concern with victims of persecution who have left their own country has been expanded to concern with internally displaced persons; UNHCR has dealt with countless refugee situations and has a staff with undeniable skill in this work. Similarly, the UN Children's Fund (UNICEF) has strong capacities for helping women and children in emergencies. The more distant World Health Organization (WHO) can offer medical expertness and, in some case, some supplies. The World Food Program (WFP) usually has stocks available for emergency feeding. UNDP can offer assessments of local conditions as a result both of its long presence in the developing countries and its chain of local offices. It can also help with short-term projects in emergencies and, with the World Bank, longer-term development.

Beyond these organizations that have their base in formal govern-mental decisions, the Secretariat maintains contact with a long list of NGOs that act in emergencies. The International Committee of the Red Cross and its sister body, the International Federation of Red Cross and Red Crescent Societies, can be invited to help. Many other NGOs eagerly offer assistance of many kinds, ranging from teaching children to read to preparing their grandparents for return to working ancestral land. Nor is the list of helpers exhausted with the UN system and the NGOs. Some governments act on their own to provide assistance in foreign emergencies. Their activities may be coordinated with the UN effort, but if they go ahead on their own, only persuasion can bring their efforts into a broader program.

All of these capacities should ideally be coordinated into a system that gets at its tasks efficiently.[30] Even getting an understanding from various participants as to what has to be done, let alone real coordina-tion, requires information, knowledge, diplomacy and energy. Whether any standing organization can achieve optimal results in such combined coordination and pleading may be doubtful and depends on the circumstances. It means persuading several international organiza-tions, governments along with their services, and NGOs to work as a team, to avoid duplication and to make serious commitments. In this process, the Secretary-General has only moral authority to convince independent organizational leaders and no ability to issue commands. Repeated experience with this task demonstrates how difficult it is to get such agreements quickly and to carry them out in tandem. Even so, patching together something that works is now an integral part of maintaining peace and therefore on the agenda of the Secretariat and the Secretary-General.

The wars in Iraq and several emergencies in Africa have put the Secretary-General and Secretariat on the front line in organizing humanitarian relief. They have also highlighted how supposedly impartial humanitarian functions both responded to and shaped polit-ical action.

After the first war in Iraq, ordained by the Security Council, the government of Saddam Hussein systematically frustrated the obser-vation of disarmament and also restricted most of the humanitarian programs ordered by the Security Council. An exception was the hurried organization of humanitarian services for the Kurdish-dominated north of Iraq, where NATO forces were brought in to maintain security. The Kurds soon established a semblance of demo-cratic self-government in the region, thus posing a constitutional issue for the eventual post-Saddam Iraq.

The response to the humanitarian needs in northern Iraq, as well as experiences in Rwanda and some other crises where direct UN involvement was less central, opened a political discussion as to the utility, legality and practicality of "humanitarian intervention". While the concept can hardly be said to have entered the accepted UN menu of responses, it nevertheless emphasizes a broadening of peace-maintaining functions.

While northern Iraq with outside help healed some of its wounds, in the rest of the country news media reported suffering among the civilian population as a result of sanctions ordered by the Security Council. Relief there was to be provided through supplies purchased with revenues from sales of oil that were supposedly strictly controlled under Security Council supervision. But reports of diversions of supplies to Saddam Hussein's purposes soon cast doubt on the operation.

Increasing frustration with the resistance of the Iraqi government to clarifying the extent of its military armory and the meticulous pace of an inspection mission[31] organized by the Security Council eventually exhausted any remaining patience in the George W. Bush government. After the United States government failed to persuade the Council to support renewed armed action, it and its "coalition" organized the second war outside UN channels. Secretary-General Annan was "out of the loop", along with the Security Council itself. He hewed to the position that the procedures specified in the UN Charter ought to be followed and eventually stated in a BBC interview in mid-2004 that, without the approval of the Security Council, the war was illegal.

Once the fighting had ended, increasing frustration with rebuilding a governing infrastructure in Iraq, along with sustained criticism from other governments in late 2003, brought the United States back to the United Nations. Secretary-General Annan had earlier withdrawn the international personnel of the UN mission – which had had only vague instructions from the Security Council as to its role – after the bombing of its office in Baghdad. Early in 2004, Annan sent Brahimi, who had headed UN affairs in Afghanistan, to Iraq at the request of the United States and the Iraqi government it had organized. Brahimi recommended, and Annan endorsed, the notion that no elections could be held at once, but rather after the end of 2004. UN expertness in managing elections was made available in Iraq.

Before then, however, the foreign military units, preponderantly from the United States and to a lesser extent from Great Britain, were increasingly subject to ambushes and explosions. Reconstruction programs were hampered and the possibility of elections encountered doubtful reactions. The United States, in at least a partial about-face, increasingly used conciliatory language and sought more consultation with the United Nations. It hoped for collaboration from its members and the Security Council and Secretary-General in dealing with the uncontrolled situation on the ground. Meanwhile, some UN humanitarian programs limped on alongside the foreign military units, but the full international component of the UN assistance teams was not yet returned before the US-led coalition turned over power to the new interim government in 2004. Imperiled by attacks, preparations went ahead for an election in January 2005 with help from a UN election assistance team.

During every phase of the UN concern with Iraq after its invasion of Kuwait, the Secretariat has had both to organize relief and to adjust to a perilous security situation. With no control over armed action, the Secretary-General participated in the preparation of decisions by the Security Council. One involved a relief program within boycotted Iraq for which oil sales paid. Proceeds from the Oil-for-Food program covered imports of food and medicine. Private contractors carried out much of the management while the Iraqi governement bought and distributed the approved supplies. Given UN staff resources and the atmosphere of suspicion, the program operated under strain. In 2004, reports of corruption led to probing investigations and demands from some sources in Washington for Annan's resignation. A detailed interim report in early 2005 by a special UN commision[32] pointed up some possible, but not large scale, corruption and serious shortcomings that Annan undertook to correct. He ordered disciplinary action against two staff members.

Persuasion and coercion

Compared with the original blueprint for the office of the Secretary-General and the staff in political and security matters, the expansion of their responsibilities could be judged as impressive. Mere breadth of mandate does not, however, measure quality of output. That has been the object of criticism from governments and observers almost from the beginning.[33] Legal and political objections arise with each application of these responsibilities, whether ordered by the Security Council or the General Assembly. Moreover, the very permanent membership of the Security Council, anchored in the world of 1945, raises questions of legitimacy and so far unmet demands for reform to provide better representation.

Part of the reason for criticism from governments of the Secretary-General's activity in peace maintenance has to do with the notion of the sovereign state. Governments do not usually accept giving up part of their authority or autonomy unless they can be convinced of very good reasons to do so. The crucial position that has sometimes been assigned to the Secretary-General therefore inherently raises questions about what is precisely intended in the questions of handling peace and security about which governments and their diplomatic representatives tend to be most sensitive.

Beyond that is the question of efficiency. Measuring efficiency poses all of the overarching questions about the precision of the mandate, the equipment of the UN as an institution, the ingenuity and zeal of the UN staff, and the degree to which governments actually carry out what they promise.

As the office of Secretary-General was designed to help with persuading governments to settle differences peacefully, the very expansion of peacekeeping and growth of the organization underlines the possibilities of controversy and possible complete or partial failure in carrying out mandates. Because some of these mandates carry substantial contributions from the Secretary-General and staff, they themselves form part of the controversy. It is hard not to conclude that it could not be otherwise.

5   Promoting global general welfare

If any part of the UN system and its basic law could be understood as optimistically turned towards bettering the condition of mankind,[1] it is the concern with economic and social cooperation. Proponents of so-called "realism" generally dismiss the aims set out in a remarkably broad part of the UN Charter[2] as utopian. Another stream of comment disagrees. It embraces the thought that higher living standards and human afflictions that cannot be confined by national boundaries can yield to international cooperation. Furthermore, promotion of human rights comprises conditions necessary for maintaining peace. From this foundation, UN institutional features, specific programs and Secretariat activities have evolved into a vast web of complex commitments, theories, expert networks and continuing activity.

Between the intellectual poles of "realism" and multilateral approaches to economic and social issues, a perhaps infinite variety of policies may be invented and debated. Yet whether or not the foundations of peace can be found in the economic and social underpinnings of human existence, clearly some continuing issues demand transnational treatment. This was, for instance, acknowledged in the nineteenth century, long before standing global machinery existed, by the general adoption of regulations to prevent sea transport from spreading plague and other epidemic diseases. In the economic sphere, preventing another disaster such as the Great Depression of 1929 would also demand the application of global policies. Meeting such needs draws wide support from governments, even if the penetration of the national realm by contemporary intergovernmental organs may not.

Although differentiating the "political" from "technical" programs of international cooperation can logically be challenged as simplistic or even naive, one part of the original UN mandate for economic and social cooperation clearly penetrates farther into the autonomy of states than the rest. This is the provision in Article 55 of the UN Charter for promotion of "universal respect for, and observance of, human rights and fundamental freedoms for all without distinction as to race, sex, language or religion". In many respects, this mandate has developed into programs that intersect activities to maintain international security. For almost every aspect of UN activity it offers a far-reaching basis, which governments may resent, especially when it is their ox that is gored.

Over the years, the Cold War conditioned and certainly limited what governments were prepared to support in the UN framework. For instance, donor governments linked their official development assistance to political support or benefits in trade from recipients. Both parties in the Cold War sought visible results to cement their support. Some of the failures – unnecessary stadiums in capitals, grand government buildings, useful factories crumbling for lack of maintenance and ill-equipped universities – still recall this era.

With the shift in UN membership from the 1960s as the colonial system expired, the hopes that the UN system could effectively stimulate and underpin economic development – but not necessarily social or governmental change – soon burgeoned. Yet the doctrines of the Cold War and the colonial struggle offered little in the way of common goals and methods. The wealthiest countries emphasized prudence, results and varied levels of support for development based on private enterprise. They were unwilling, as their domestic voices sometimes put it, to sign "blank checks". Generally, however, the developing-countries-organized "non-aligned movement" (NAM) of the Cold War, hewed to a line which insisted on broad government participation and national, rather than international, decision-making. Even so, the underlying political results of decolonization inevitably bred institutional change and adaptation. Some of the changes had strong Secretariat backing and all affected its work.

The long-term nature of most of what is done under the title of economic and social cooperation, however, demands less immediate attention from the Secretary-General than crisis-driven issues of peace maintenance. A great deal of the Secretariat works at long-term issues of economic and social cooperation (excluding human rights) rather than with so-called "political" questions. Aside from the services for all activities, economic and social programs require nearly double what the UN spends on direct "political affairs".[3]

The Secretary-General does routinely offer at the opening of the two annual sessions of the UN Economic and Social Council (ECOSOC) an analytical statement which the economic and social specialists of the Secretariat shape. It always gives an overview of the state of UN economic and social cooperation and its implications.

The economic and social department of the Secretariat usually operates, along with other partners in the UN system, with little notice in the media that reach the mass public. Its subject matter involves technical content to which the output of the Secretariat contributes, sometimes crucially, sometimes marginally, frequently invisibly. Yet its agenda also touches on poignant human problems, including refugees and migration, the trade in narcotic drugs, crime, and the suppression of traffic in women and children. The ultimate results stand or fall in response to national governmental decisions to comply with recommendations and may remain almost unnoticed outside of governmental and expert circles. Thus, technical concerns bear on political decisions on the part of governments.

This chapter will begin with an examination of the role of the Secretariat in the formation of global policy on economic and social issues and go on to a treatment of cooperation on human rights. It will include examples, but far less than a comprehensive survey, of the practices and work in this area and will seek to explain the opportunities and limitations of leadership in this realm.

Global policy

ECOSOC provides a convenient vantage point from which to scan the way in which the officials of the Secretariat contribute to the development of global policy that is ultimately decided by the General Assembly. By nature, these processes mostly employ abstract statements that signal to the majority of UN member governments at least rhetorical agreement that they ought to apply universally. When it works at its best, ECOSOC mirrors the application of the policies that it had recommended via the General Assembly to all members. Intrinsically then, the aim of global polices to promote the general welfare is the establishment of base lines, recommending lines of response and evaluating results. Governments advance, if they do not entirely ignore, these base lines with decisions and programs that have different rates of application, depending on local conditions, and different outcomes. Consequently critics of the process who expect highly disciplined responses and quick results dismiss it as a waste of time and effort.

The annual session of ECOSOC in July is devoted to substantive issues. ECOSOC itself, enlarged from its original 18 elected governments to 54, is too large for give-and-take debate. Although the membership is made up from geographical groups in the General Assembly, the Permanent Members of the Security Council can count on election. But the geographical base practically guarantees representation from governments with very mixed capacities to contribute to the discussion and to execute the policies they approve. Moreover, its agenda is seen by many traditional diplomats, who concentrate on security issues, as secondary and worth only derision. Consequently, some governments send relatively inexpert junior representatives. The deficit in authoritative representation is partly made up by a brief "high-level segment" of each session in which more senior governmental representatives participate. Nevertheless, all of the broad divisions in world politics, including the Cold War, the demise of colonialism, the desirability of state versus private enterprise, the status of human rights, the problems associated with state debt, and much more, affect everything that ECOSOC does.

If the size of ECOSOC and the intellectual preparation and rank of national representatives condition its debate, it is further complicated, constrained and augmented by other participants. Each of the 14 largely autonomous Specialized Agencies associated in the UN system reports to the Council. These agencies range in institutional size from the slender World Intellectual Property Organization to the massive World Bank. All have their own intergovernmental decisional bodies. Their scope runs from hundreds of field projects in developing countries to narrow, attenuated expert networks operated from quiet offices and sedate intergovernmental councils in Geneva. In addition, the 11 mainly operating organizations created by the General Assembly, including the UNHCR, UNHCHR, UNICEF, the UN Development Programme (UNDP), the World Food Programme (WFP), the UN Population Fund (UNFPA), the UN Environment Programme (UNEP) and more, report on their activities to ECOSOC. All of these organizations send representatives who may present statements to Council and participate in discussions.

As the ECOSOC was planned and has operated primarily as an intergovernmental organ to coordinate and produce and supervise global policy, its effectiveness would partly grow out of profound research and advice on the issues on its agenda. The device of expert advisory bodies, used by the League of Nations, was therefore incorporated in the UN system. This provided for the creation of so-called functional commissions, only one of which, that on human rights, was specified in Article 68 of the UN Charter. From an ideologically driven compromise between forming commissions from governmental representatives or independent experts, the membership is now made up of persons who are nominated by governments, presumably because of their expertness. After various changes over the years, eight of these bodies, now advise ECOSOC on population, statistics, social development, narcotic drugs, the status of woman, crime, science and technology, and sustainable development. The governments asked to nominate members are designated by a formula of geographical distribution and their numbers vary between 24 and 53.[4] The quality of the resulting advice and the degree to which it actually influences governmental policy and the recommendations of the ECOSOC varies greatly with the touchiness of the issues involved and the personal capacities of the members. The geographical basis of membership combined with governmental nominations makes it obvious that these commissions are far from the original idea of independent minds brought together exclusive for objective advice.

The ECOSOC is also the only UN organ that has a formal mandate that opens the way to direct contact with the civil society. This is set out in the UN Charter as the possibility of consulting with non-governmental organizations (NGOs).[5] This possibility blossomed over the years into a list of more than 2,000 organizations and an increasingly close partnership between some of the most persuasive of the NGOs and government representatives during proceedings in the Council. Some of these organizations serve as a source of authoritative information and advice to ECOSOC, its commissions and the Secretariat. Human rights organizations have a particularly close, beyond a strictly formalized, relationship with the UN human rights machinery.

Every part of this institutional complexity makes demands on the UN Secretariat for documents, analysis, reports and research. As some of the agenda items continue under instructions from the ECOSOC from year to year, a considerable degree of routine churning of the same facts and ideas ensues and finds its way into largely ignored papers. Members of the Secretariat who work on such reporting very quickly become the rare experts on what specific activities the UN and member governments undertake as a result of ECOSOC decisions. They can consequently insert a particular tone in the proceedings and on many occasions quietly inject their thoughts or take the initiative in offering government representatives ideas and data for mapping an altered or, for that matter, unchanged course. They not only compile the institutional memory but themselves embody the bureaucratic memory – the sum of their personal experience – of UN work for the general welfare. Moreover, ECOSOC decisions, recommendations and practices gave rise to much periodical publishing, including such examples as information on the status of women, the problems associated with water and the execution of economic development measures brought forth by global conferences.

More than 30 global conferences on economic and social issues were summoned by the United Nations between 1970 and the turn of the new century.[6] Although these conferences do not escape criticism, the "conference system that was progressively developed by the United Nations is an integral part of its existence".[7] In some respects, they responded to the widespread uneasiness over the performance of the ECOSOC, for they brought together representatives of almost all UN member governments in a format that had expert preparation and increasing participation from the civic society. Since the global conference on the environment in 1972, that topic never vanished from the UN agenda. Three conferences took up the issues posed by population, including control, migration and aging. Four conferences were devoted to the condition of women; this was a topic that, like population, had sharply barbed aspects in some societies. Other conferences dealt with human rights, children, refugees, energy, water and desertification, food, health and AIDS. When topics were repeatedly taken up, each conference reflected experience. It offered changing knowledge, adjusted theories and new recommendations, some of them a shrill recitation of what governments had failed to do.

Global conferences, whether stimulated by the Secretariat, as some are, or the result of governmental initiative, demand special efforts. The resources of the Secretariat may be augmented with extra personnel and above all by drawing on expert networks in the subject matter. Although governments ultimately decide on the content of the conferences as well as the participants and expected outcome, others are consulted. Known by network participants, including Secretariat members, the outside specialists, who may be located in government services, academia, research institutes and other international agencies, prepare searching papers to define and support agenda items. Further feelers go out to NGOs with interests appropriate for the conference. The outcome is usually a declaration setting out a program to which governments are urged to commit themselves and to act accordingly. A specific endorsement by the General Assembly makes it officially a UN conference. To these, too, the Secretariat officials who develop and manage the conferences usually contribute ideas, rhetoric and persuasion as well as building the agenda. However diligent the preparation, some of these conferences have nevertheless ended in frustration and bitterness.

Coordinating the UN system

The United Nations system is anything but monolithic. Its diverse components need to line up in the same direction for it to have anything like systematic form in approaching global policies that cut across economic and social sectors.

Whether it is desirable or not, this lack of unity owes much to the application of the concept of functionalism that strongly influenced the creation of international organization after World War II.[8] It held essentially that transnational issues could be successfully dealt with by specialists and experts who would eschew "politics". So the national officials who dealt with public health or telecommunications, for instance, could reach agreements that technologically-ignorant politicians never could. Thus, the way to a peaceful world lay through cooperation based on expertness.

Even before the League of Nations, some functional organizations had proved successful. The League of Nations picked up the techniques used in these organizations and extended them, but despite the founders' intentions, it never became the center of all such cooperation. Its associated International Labor Organization (ILO) did, however, represent a large addition to the functional framework. The League also created a formal structure for public health issues.

The experience with functional agencies convinced the planners of the United Nations that decentralized operations would serve peace and welfare better than one central organization. Consequently by the time that United Nations itself formally came into being, close cooperation was expected with the Universal Postal Union, the International Telegraphic (later Telecommunications) Union and the ILO, all of which had survived World War II. To their ranks would soon be added the International Civil Aviation Organization (ICAO), Food and Agriculture Organization (FAO), the UN Educational, Scientific and Cultural Organization (UNESCO), World Health Organization (WHO). the World Bank (WB) and the International Monetary Fund (IMF). All of these were planned while the United Nations itself took tentative form.[9] They were the subject of international constitutional conferences like the founding conference of the United Nations.

The UN pattern of their own foundation laws, states members, periodic policy-making meetings of members, contributed finances, a chief officer and a secretariat were features of the new agencies. This meant that they would operate autonomously although linked by formal agreements to the United Nations. They maintain contacts with the substantive national ministries, such as labor, communications and the treasury that parallel the UN access to foreign affairs ministries.

This mode of organizing international cooperation obviously did not automatically put the pieces of policy decisions by governments and the United Nations into a tidy pattern. The issues involved in public health, for instance, had a relationship to economic development to which the World Bank would give attention. Nor could the concerns of the labor force, the subject of ILO deliberation, simply be pushed aside when considering economic programs or human rights. The issue of efficient organization of the work of these Specialized Agencies, as the UN Charter referred to them, then, could be encapsulated in that rather elastic bureaucratic term "coordination".

The ECOSOC was given the mandate in Articles 57 and 63 of the UN Charter to strive for coordinating the work of these organizations. This was to be based on the formal agreements made with the agencies about reporting and participation in the ECOSOC discussion. The ECOSOC could make recommendations but not issue orders to these autonomous organizations. Indeed the World Bank and the IMF took great pains to make agreements that protected their distance from interference by the ECOSOC which they considered too political for financial operations. The Secretariat had a direct hand in working out these agreements which also were made with the organizations that later were founded.

A few persuasive members of the Secretariat when ECOSOC first met had experienced the pioneering efforts of the League of Nations in functionalist organization. They were ready, if they had not suggested it, to support the creation of what was known with fine bureaucratic draftsmanship as the Administrative Committee on Coordination (ACC).[10] It has now been succeeded by the Chief Executives Board for Coordination (CEB) of Annan's time. ACC's original four members have grown to representatives of 27 international organizations. Taken together, they stand for the UN system, even though the World Bank and the IMF differentiate themselves from the other autonomous UN Specialized Agencies and from the organizations, such as UNICEF, established by the General Assembly.

ACC and its successor can be understood as the forum for the dukes of the UN system. It is presided over by the Secretary-General. He has, however, no power to issue directives to the represented organizations. Some, such as WFP, have very large field programs and others, such as the World Bank, dispose of impressive resources for development. All of them depend on support within the relevant ministries of the member governments of their organizations. CEB includes no governmental representatives. It does report on its work to ECOSOC and the General Assembly.

CEB now marks out methods for coordinating the work of the various agencies around themes, such as energy and water or financing development. Such themes cut across all or most of the work of the member agencies. It also tries to find common ground on administrative policies that affect their staffs and their relations with each other. A staff for CEB is provided by the UN Secretariat. It provides papers for consideration and services for meeting, much in the style that intergovernmental sessions operate.

CEB seeks, in the style of adjacent feudal lords settling boundaries, means of concerting their activities so that they add up to more, not less. Some of its members, who are chief executives or senior staff members, take part in decisions, such as granting loans or providing shelter for refugees, that are important to governments. Although some members' voices have more weight than others, the sessions necessarily emphasize persuasion and mutual advantages. At the same time, agreements among the agency heads can result in concerted attention in policy organs throughout the UN system. The leadership of the UN Secretary-General in reaching such agreements or stimulating new approaches to long-term issues can be telling, both in terms of policy and his own persuasiveness.

Innovative economic analysis

To claim that the UN Secretariat or its individual members were the exclusive source of what the governments represented on ECOSOC or the General Assembly accepted as economic wisdom would simply ignore how collaboration in research networks elaborates ideas. If cooperation in the UN system did anything with these ideas, it certainly brought them before governmental representatives in UN organs. Ideas then would, if the process were to succeed, work their way into and through governmental policy mechanisms and resurface as support for propositions that Secretariat members had presented. By the end of the first 20 years of the UN, it was clear that much of the activity of the UN system had to do with economic development. That meant in essence, UN activity and programs were aimed at and accepted by the great majority of member governments, whether or not they were adequately carried out.

"As always," a pioneering study of UN ideas points out, "the role of specific individuals in the UN was crucial".[11] These included two Nobel prize winners in economics – Sir W. Arthur Lewis and Gunnar

Myrdal – and such leading figures as Professor Hans Singer, a tireless stimulator of discourse on the economy. They used the UN in the early days as an amplifier for the neglected study of economic development. In the enthusiastic atmosphere of the times, these soon became the theoretical basis for practical approaches.[12]

Three pioneering reports turned over to ECOSOC by the Secretary-General "also pioneered a pattern. Each was prepared by a team of prominent economists from different parts of the world, with support from the UN Secretariat".[13] These reports covered measures to promote full employment, mentioned in Article 55 of the Charter but regarded in Washington as a controversial notion, as well as approaches to economic development and stability. They differed in emphasis and method from textbook economics of the time and moderated the emphasis on growth via the market that strongly influenced the United States and other rich country policies. The reports clearly marked out methods, projected novel notions and later fitted with the way that the stream of new members from the developing world would look for UN leadership in economic development.

At the same time, encouraged by the United States' proposals for practical help for development, the Secretariat put together a program of technical assistance for governments that asked for it. This was based on the expectation that strategic advice – "know how" in the jargon of the times – would quickly stimulate development. With leadership from senior figures in the Secretariat, initial agencies were gradually transformed into what is now UNDP. The Secretariat at UN headquarters and in the regional economic commissions also still offer some technical assistance.

The conceptual approaches that ECOSOC and the General Assembly accepted as the key to economic development[14] changed with experience and criticism, much of it directed toward the World Bank and the IMF as well as to the UN itself. These changes, some of them coming to maturity only after decades of expert debate, are represented in short titles. These included global planning, in the UN context driven by another Nobel Prize winner, Jan Tinbergen, a Dutch academic.[15] This was succeeded by basic human needs, then by sustainable economic development, itself incorporating attention to the protection of the environment, and reduction of poverty. In addition, much more emphasis was given to the social and environmental consequences of development and to human rights. In all of the detailed theoretical discussions that underlay these mutations, the UN Secretariat had a voice and at times a leading part. Its own analytical capacities were increasingly complemented and soon indeed overshadowed by the research of UNDP, UNICEF, the World Bank, IMF, ILO and such important extra-UN bodies as the Organisation for Economic Co-operation and Development (OECD), which enlisted the wealthy countries, and the European Union. By participating in the expert networks, units of the Secretariat drew inspiration or background knowledge for their own reports.

Institutional mutations

If a glance backwards over the UN-centered cooperation on global issues seems more eclectic than focused, that certainly was not the intention that drove some of the institutional mutation. The existence of the five regional commissions on economic and social issues[16] suggests a tension between a hierarchic and decentralized system. Although considerable doubts accompanied their foundation under ECOSOC auspices, their proponents successfully argued that neighbors understood each other better than distant councils and that they shared problems that might be efficiently solved together. The doubts continued to emerge from time to time as the commissions, whose staff members are part of the UN Secretariat, represent considerable expense and the usual management troubles of a decentralized system. Nevertheless, "regional commissions," writes a close observer, "have played an important and useful role in the realm of ideas".[17]

One of the most celebrated of these ideas emerged from the UN Economic Commission for Latin America and the Caribbean (ECLAC)[18] in studies beginning in the late 1940s; it laid the basis for what became the UN Conference on Trade and Development (UNCTAD), now a permanent agency responsible to the General Assembly. The underlying theoretical package, was designed mainly by Raúl Prebisch, the ECLAC executive director. He argued in publications of the commission and elsewhere that outside the rich nucleus of developed countries, the poorer ones on the periphery were held back by decisions beyond their control.[19] Their dependence on markets for commodities and on arbitrary movements of capital created what might be termed a global class system of rich and poor – or, in the words of the time, a center-periphery dependency relationship.

To remedy this inequality, Prebisch proposed creating a bargaining mechanism through which fairer prices and more efficient capital movements might be achieved. The rich countries, the socialist (at the time, the Soviet bloc) lands and the then 77 developing nations would confer, reach bargains with the wealthy lands and sponsor permanent measures to diminish the inequalities by such devices as price stability for commodities. With determination, persistence and sophisticated arguments, Prebisch and his supporters among governments finally overcame resistance to calling the first Conference on Trade and Development in 1964.[20] It began with a temporary secretariat and eventually developed into today's permanent UNCTAD with its own senior executive, appointed by the UN Secretary-General, intergovernmental council and budget. It left a still visible ideological mark in the rather feebly functioning Group of 77.

Although the global bargain foreseen by Prebisch never eventuated either inside or outside the UN environment, UNCTAD's genesis as a critic of the free-market, growth-oriented World Bank and IMF proved a rationale for its continuous existence.[21] Its Secretariat steadily developed analytical capacities, especially of the flow of international investment, that could not be ignored and gradually became an integral part of the broadening policy consensus in the UN system. In its periodic plenary sessions, it still receives rhetorical support from the Group of 77, as well as criticism from the developed group, even if in most respects it has become only one voice in a complex discourse.

If the grander aspirations of the UNCTAD movement largely remain as shadows in the research aimed largely at governments and civil servants, another related and even more grandiose attempt to reshape the world economy left less in the way of markers in the UN system. UNCTAD research and advocacy contributed to it. This was the attempt by the Group of 77 and the overlapping NAM to use the United Nations to impose a New International Economic Order (NIEO). Its immediate inspiration came out of the petroleum boycott and the success of the Organization of Petroleum-Exporting Countries (OPEC) during the 1973 war between Israel and its neighbors to use cartel methods to dominate the market.

After a bitter debate between the developed and developing countries, with the socialist bloc offering side bets, the majority of the General Assembly in a special session in 1974 adopted a lengthy declaration calling for NIEO and later a law-making treaty that had little effect. It represented an attempt fundamentally to reorganize world markets in commodities and give them specific direction. This notion immediately encountered unrelenting hostility from the backers of free markets which the United States led.

Whatever the merits of the idea, the decisions of the General Assembly were mandates for the Secretariat. The Assembly ordered the rearrangement of priorities on economic cooperation to give effect to NIEO. A paramount Director-General (now abolished) in the

Secretariat was appointed to pull every part of the work into line with NIEO. The same aspirations were put to the entire UN family in forceful terms, so that every organization associated with ECOSOC was obliged to react at least rhetorically.

From the high point of the special session of the Assembly and the appointment of the Director-General, the entire approach glided with increasing speed into obscurity. It encountered opposition within parts of the Secretariat and, of course, the World Bank and IMF. To the US government, it represented economic heresy. Its theoretical assumptions proved too controversial to follow for practical programs. Nevertheless, mandates are mandates in public bureaucracies. The UN Secretariat responded, if not always with maximum zeal, with the customary reports, structural accommodations and recommendations. By the new century, almost all of this had become drips from the vat of history.

Both UNCTAD and the NIEO could be read as attempts to institutionalize via the UN process and to push ahead with specific, rather ideological, approaches to economic development. Institutionalization, it was hoped by the supporters, would offer an effective means of ensuring continuing attention to a topic. In the event, UNCTAD and NIEO had discernible immediate effects on the Secretariat, but only the former adapted to the changing international mood.

Environment and development

A quite different result emerged from gradually increasing awareness of the need to protect the global environment. Here, direct impulse came from the world of NGOs whose agitation about pollution, climate change and the decline of biodiversity combined with governmental interest, spearheaded by Sweden, to engender a world conference on the subject. The results of the Stockholm conference on the environment of 1972 meant that the environmental consequences of economic activity and development gradually permeated the UN system. The outcomes were monitored by the United Nations Environment Programme (UNEP), a new organization formally established by the General Assembly and soon financed, if never with noteworthy generosity, by member governments.

Two decades later an even bigger conference in Rio de Janeiro reviewed results and staked out new and more comprehensive directions.[22] There, for the first time, the interest and effects of the growing relationship of the UN and representatives of the civic society took on dramatic proportions. Thousands of NGO representatives turned up and more than ever before were not only welcomed by the meeting but had a substantial share in working out the gigantic final document in an explicit way that linked the environment with development. It set out directions for the entire UN system, the results of which became evident, for instance, in obligatory environmental impact studies in relation to proposed World Bank and UNDP projects.

In many ways, the conference was driven by a UN insider, Maurice Strong, a Canadian who as a young man had served as a guard in UN headquarters and later had filled senior positions in the Secretariat. His experience included service in business and public organizational posts in Canada and as Secretary-General of the Stockholm environmental conference. He was called back to shape the Rio Conference.[23] His broad vision and knowledge of the UN system helped to mobilize its expertness on economic development and to profit from the specialist networks. The resulting declaration of the conference again permeated the entire UN system and stimulated NGO and governmental activity. It created standing mechanisms for observing changes in the global environment and for institutionalizing protective measures and standards for development that had not only desirable economic but also environmental results. It resulted in the creation of the ECOSOC's Commission on Sustainable Development with expansion of contact with NGOs and an agenda that cut across earlier definitions. Still, the wide program of international cooperation and national action, in which environmental considerations would balance and support economic development in the developing countries, hardly achieved anything like the hoped-for maximum effect. Moreover, important cooperation among governments to reduce the warming effects on the global environment of using fossil fuels was eventually rejected by the United States, by far the biggest consumer.

In many respects, the Stockholm conference, and especially the follow-up in Rio, in an obvious, not to say demonstrative, form drew on the accretion of knowledge and expertness in the UN system. The subject matter – newly articulated concerns about the environment combined with the familiar but unsatisfied search of development of the poorer lands – was displayed in NGO activity as essential, pressing and worthy of wide concern. Leadership in the conference by Strong and his staff, which drew on the officials of the UN system, was unmistakable.

Financing for development

A decade later, another conference began to grow out of a quiet mining of the UN system on a more technical topic that had similar refractory political implications. It resulted in the Monterrey Conference of 2003 on financing economic development.

The topic of financing for development long figured in UN Secretariat research and in often strident debate in the General Assembly since the 1950s. The notion of active discussion leading to a policy conclusion to which the donor governments would agree always encountered opposition. However, in the aftermath of the Asian economic crisis that began in 1997 in Thailand, the American delegate in the economic committee of General Assembly without fanfare indicated a change of opinion. This was immediately seized upon by an energetic Mexican representative who began a diplomatic round and a process towards a General Assembly resolution. These included persuading the World Bank and the IMF, as well as several governments, of the possible benefits. It eventuated in the Monterrey (Mexico) Conference in 2003 where President Vincente Fox of Mexico and President George W. Bush, who had just met in the Mexican capital, were participants along with heads of state or of governments from more than 50 countries and more than 200 ministers of various government departments.

UN Secretariat officials, including the Secretary-General, were deeply involved in the preparations for the conference and were often consulted about the negotiations, but their role was primarily technical, supportive and facilitative. The background of decades of UN research, planning and advising, bearing on the negotiations that hewed closer to the normal diplomatic model than technical economic enquiry, made a contribution to the preparation for the conference. At the conference itself, following the usual pattern of world conferences, the Secretariat managed the arrangements and advised on the procedure.

In the end the Monterrey conferees, who adopted a relatively short final declaration, heard the American president promise an addition of $5 billion to its contribution to economic development by 2006. Other governments added their intentions. Not all of this, of course, would be directed through the UN system and, indeed, legislative action would still be required in many countries. The governments, however, for the first time gave their collective assent to serious measures to expand development financing. Whatever the long-term effect of these commitments may be, the conference demonstrated how the capacities of the international institutions and their staff members could help advance the formulation of a policy and the monitoring of its application.

At the same time, the outcome of the Monterrey Conference has probably shifted the center of gravity for policy analysis and advocacy away from the UN Secretariat to Washington. There, the staff capacities of the World Bank and the International Monetary Fund, as well as the neighboring US Treasury, can be engaged.

Human rights

The several mentions of human rights in the UN Charter could be taken as an index of expectations. The topic was placed under the wings of ECOSOC, itself mandated to work outside the "political" realm of maintaining security. In the prevailing temper of the times at the end of World War II, "technical" matters were thought to be separable from the real "political" agenda assigned to the Security Council. Yet within three years a document emerged from the Commission on Human Rights (CHR) of ECOSOC that on the face of it had far reaching significance for governmental behavior. This was the Universal Declaration of Human Rights, adopted by the General Assembly in 1948 with near perfect assent and no negative vote. If the memoirs of the first Secretary-General were taken as a barometer,[24] the Declaration was worth only incidental notice amidst the details of now half-forgotten Cold War maneuvers where the Security Council's work at best had a minor effect. The roots of the Declaration reached back to the still fresh horror of the Nazi racial policies and still farther to earlier humanitarian law-making. It also had strong backing from the United States, whose effective delegate to the commission was Eleanor Roosevelt, the widow of the late president.

In fact, the new document proved not only pioneering in its scope and content but also opened a continuing preoccupation that in both rhetoric and some policies has diffused through the UN system. Probably many governments that voted for a mere "Declaration" underestimated the significance of what could easily have been taken as a harmless bit of diplomatic fluff.

Because the Declaration purported to set a standard for the treatment by governments of their citizens, the legislative and executive process it began had anything but a merely technical content. It called on governments to guarantee such familiar – at least in the Western democracies – civil rights as freedom of speech, assembly and worship and prohibition of arbitrary arrest, torture, detention or exile, guarantee of the security of persons and entitlement to rights without racial, sex, political or other discrimination. As if these were not prescriptions enough to make many governments uneasy or hostile, the Declaration also sought guarantees of the right ownership of property, the right to take part in government, to work and protection from unemployment, equal pay for equal work, leisure, periodic holidays, education, participation in cultural life, and in Article 28 even "a social and international order in which the rights and freedoms set forth in [the] Declaration can be fully realized". The application, or even making claims, of such rights as these would now be treated as it was then by some – perhaps many indeed – governments as seditious and revolutionary. Their reactions would have been sound.

Yet even in an organization of sovereign states whose governments could be counted on usually to resist encroachments on their autonomy, a legislative process involving the CHR, ECOSOC and the General Assembly, and ultimately national governments, has projected proposals of new international law to which most states in the world have adhered. These include the legally binding Covenants on Civil and Political Rights and on Economic and Social Rights, that required a dozen years of negotiation. The Convention on Genocide that was drafted at the same time as the Declaration on Human Rights has also received very wide adherence. Some governments, like the United States, attached reservations of various kinds to the human rights covenants and Washington has declined to accept the economic and social convention. Later these basic documents were followed by widely accepted conventions such as those on the rights of women, against racial discrimination, and one on rights of children that was ratified by every UN member except Somalia and the United States.

The UN Secretariat constantly offered crucial help, technical legal and drafting skills, and institutional and bureaucratic memory during the process. This included large doses of leadership by some of the early directors of the Secretariat division engaged in serving the CHR, the principal nucleus of drafting work.[25] Except in a very general *pro forma* style, the Secretary-General left it to his juniors in the staff to carry along the development of human rights law. Indeed, Pérez de Cuéllar made a point of declining to renew the contract of Theo van Boven, the director of the human rights office, after several Latin American governments protested the official's zeal in promoting the application of the laws and their extension. His first two successors followed a steadily less energetic course.

Yet, at about the same time, Pérez de Cuéllar told an Oxford University audience that human rights "are of urgent concern … This is one of my daily preoccupations and a major anxiety".[26] But he also noted the caution imposed by sensitive governments that would treat "an indiscreet intervention" with "the opposite of the desired effect … and only aggravate the suffering of the persecuted". His predecessor, Waldheim, detailed in his memoir precisely such discreet interventions, consistent with diplomatic practice, with governments, especially during visits to their countries.[27] During Waldheim's tenure, the newly-elected American president, Jimmy Carter, made the promotion and protection of human rights a centerpiece of his policy, thus pushing the entire subject much higher on the international agenda. At the same time, the repeated challenges by both the General Assembly and eventually the Security Council to the apartheid policy of South Africa made obvious the link between security policies and human rights. It was not, however, until Annan took office that the Secretary-General offered prominent public support to the human rights movements that had spread with much encouragement to NGOs to almost every part of the world.

Meantime, the several controversies inherent in human rights gradually contributed to a general reform of the Secretariat dealing with the subject. The human rights specialists had pushed along the early elaboration of the system of human rights law that came to be accepted almost unanimously by the expanding UN membership. But the sessions of the Human Rights Commission (HRC) steadily added duties, including preparation of rosters of complaints, service for *rapporteurs* on specific questions and technical aid to governments. New conventions also added monitoring duties and substantive services for meetings. To cope with all of this, the Geneva secretariat was neither large enough nor offered enough depth. Furthermore, the Commission itself was notoriously riven by disputes arising from attempts by, for instance, the United States to gain approval for criticism of China and moves to criticize the United States because of the continued use of capital punishment. A stream of criticism also came from NGOs that increasingly became an integral part of the UN program. All of this built an atmosphere in the General Assembly for much diplomatic complaint but not necessarily for an optimal Secretariat role.[28]

A focus for reform was the proposal – supported by many NGOs and some governments including, after a time, the United States – to create the post of UN High Commissioner for Human Rights (UNHCHR). Eventually the Geneva human rights secretariat became part of the office of UNHCHR, consolidating the entire range of services to governments and promotion under one head. The first High Commissioner, José Ayalo Lasso, former foreign minister of Ecuador, who was appointed by Pérez de Cuéllar, hewed to the discrete practices of diplomatic interventions. Annan appointed the former president of Ireland, Mary Robinson, as the second occupant of the post. She made it clear from the beginning that she intended to follow an activist policy.

Whatever her intentions, the conventional restraints favored by governments that resented outside criticism or thought their own policies beyond improvement affected Commissioner Robinson. Making her disquiet public, but not stilling her critical rhetoric, she announced that she sought no reappointment. To the clear relief of some governments, including the United States which "had become disillusioned with her",[29] the successor, the late Sergio Vieira de Mello, had a gentler but successful diplomatic reputation; his service was cut short by his death in Iraq. He was succeeded in 2004 by Louise Arbour of Canada.

Meanwhile, Annan, more than his predecessors, referred to human rights as a guide to policy. Human rights, he insisted, should be "mainstreamed" through the UN system. "Throughout my term as Secretary-General," he declared when the United Nations received the Nobel Peace Prize in 2001, "I have sought to place human beings at the centre of everything we do – from conflict prevention to development to human rights. Securing real and lasting improvement in the lives of individual men and women is the measure of all we do at the United Nations."[30]

Moreover, Annan emphasized, as did the top governmental leaders at the Millennium Assembly of 2000, the importance of the promotion of democracy. Along with his approach to human dignity that underlies the concept of human rights, Annan has reiterated that it is necessary "to look beyond the framework of States, and beneath the surface of nations or communities ... The sovereignty of States must no longer be used as a shield for gross violations of human rights."[31]

Annan has also made statements calling attention to specific violations of human rights in UN member countries. In 2004, for example, he reacted to reports that Sudan violated human rights and produced refugees in its Darfur province. He supported a human rights mission to investigate there. At the same time, he announced that a senior adviser on genocide would be appointed in his office to draw up an action plan that would engage the entire UN system to prevent genocide.[32] In his announcement, he also referred specific to the Rwanda genocide.

Criminal courts

In response to reports of obvious violations of human rights, of possible genocide and the parallel provisions of humanitarian law, the Security Council has organized international tribunals to deal with complaints in former Yugoslavia, Rwanda and Sierra Leone. Political and military leaders were arrested, tried before highly qualified judges appointed to benches set up in the Netherlands, Tanzania and Sierra

Leone. While the law that is applied partly derives from UN conventions, it also relies on international humanitarian law that developed through the Red Cross movement. The tribunals, however, are independent of the UN human rights machinery.

The concern with the human devastation that results from violations of human rights law also led the General Assembly to summon an international conference in 1998 in Rome to consider creating an international criminal court. The draft convention had been prepared by the International Law Commission, a sub-organ of the General Assembly. The draft approved in the Rome gathering by 120 states was soon ratified by more than 100 governments. Consequently, the tribunal was formally established in 2003 in the Netherlands. The United States, China, Israel and India, among a few others, oppose this activity and have declined to support either the convention or the court.

A reflection on human rights in the UN system

Human rights law, which rests on the extensive set of international conventions drafted and approved in UN organs,[33] provides an elaborate system of rules for governmental behavior that formally applies in much of the world. But while individuals may seek to make moral claims based on these standards, the law depends on how governments give it effect. Under Article 56 of the UN Charter, they are pledged to "take joint and separate action" to achieve the purposes of economic and social cooperation, including human rights.

If they give it no, or only partial, effect, the limits of UN machinery soon come into view. The Secretary-General, the UNHCHR and the staff can formally or informally try to get the large Commission on Human Rights or one of its sub-organs to stimulate the "naming and shaming" of offenders, or another government can do this. But given the heterogeneous membership of CHR, which invariably includes obvious violators of the standards, the outcome can hardly be judged as dependable or, as in the view of some critics, worth the expense. Even if CHR agrees that the situation is such that an investigation is needed, the suspected government can throw up obstacles and block access. That guarantees a report which raises questions more easily than it gives answers.

Senior UN officials, including the Secretary-General and UNHCHR, can issue statements and criticize governments in speeches inside and outside the UN system. In circumstances such as a threat of genocide, they may even activate the Security Council to prevent another debacle of Rwandan stripe. But they may thus spend the political capital needed for effectiveness in other situations that respond more easily than a government intent on tyrannical behavior.

The UN human rights offices can also offer services to governments wanting to upgrade their own systems. This includes the promotion of democracy, better handling of complaints, observation of elections and improving legal services generally. Yet a government has to request such services. Even with a request, UN resources offer only modest, if sometimes crucial, services.

The entire system of promoting compliance with the human rights laws and assisting willing governments has suffered from a chronic lack of money. A recent doubling of its provision left it with 2 percent of the UN budget. The Geneva human rights center has the first obligation of meeting a growing number of tasks imposed by intergovernmental organs. It is too thinly staffed even to carry these out without incurring complaints about inefficiency. Similarly, its advisory services and research are limited. NGOs voluntarily take up some of this slack, which does little to put more sinews in official UN responses to opportunities for promoting the system.

Despite all this, the rhetoric of human rights has entered political discourse almost everywhere in the world, even where governments try to stamp it out. The system thus provides the basis for claims by citizens against deprivations of their rights by governments. It offers a device for judging progress in reaching a higher standard which, whether they intend it so or not, most governments have offered.

Inside the UN system, after hesitation, development agencies now take some interest in the human rights consequences of their programs. These, too, inherently support the claims that people may make about their rights to economic and social protection and advancement. Around the UN system, and to some extent through lobbying and publicity, human rights NGOs along with many concentrating on development have sponsored grass-roots organizing efforts. These have resulted in various claims for enforcement of human rights. Whether these claims could be substantially advanced by a stronger international civil service dealing with human rights has never been adequately tested. The reactions to the first activist UNHCHR make clear that many governments oppose making that test. All the same, as the twenty-first century dawned some reactions to the genocide in Rwanda and the humanitarian disasters of Sierra Leone, Liberia and (Democratic Republic of) the Congo supported UN "humanitarian intervention" that would include coercion to sustain human rights.

6   Reaching out to broader publics

The institutional position of the Secretary-General at the summit of the Secretariat and his steady involvement with the decisional process in other organs opens the way to both policy and administrative initiatives. Yet the political aims of the UN members constrain him. The design of the UN Charter clearly implies that governments, not broad publics, must get primary attention. But each occupant of the office in bold or cloaked ways has taken noteworthy initiatives on both existing conflicts and long-term global policies. Some of these were highly public or related to issues well beyond conventional diplomatic agendas. The outcomes varied from rejection to accepted leadership. Furthermore, some of these initiatives have involved reaching out to increasingly broad publics.

This chapter takes up initiatives by Secretaries-General that on the basis of wide public notice and support were intended to stimulate or shape policies to be carried out by the member governments as well as the Secretariat. It treats the use and means of communications, including those operated by the Secretariat, to some of the publics within and outside the UN decisional structures.

Early development

During the infancy and adolescence of the United Nations, a period that coincided with some of the highest tensions of the Cold War, the Secretaries-General sought both to augment their persuasiveness as well as to set organizational precedents. The nature of the Cold War usually blocked them from much direct effect on the Soviet Union and United States, the dominant contending pair.

An early initiative by Lie involving the then vexed question of the representation of China in the United Nations gave notice of how governments might react to avoid precedents. In 1948, Lie asked his legal department for a paper on which government – the Kuomintang in Taiwan or the Communists in Beijing – had the right to take the Chinese seat in the Security Council and the General Assembly. The advice given by Lie and communicated to the Council, which had not asked for it, found that the Beijing government had the better case. The Kuomintang ambassador, who occupied the veto-bearing Chinese place, furiously opposed this initiative.[1] Lie had little support for his conclusions from other members and on political grounds certainly not then from the United States or the other Western governments. The reaction failed to establish a right of the Secretary-General formally to inject legal opinions on the agenda of the Council. Moreover, it made clear that legal arguments do not drive its political decisions.

Lie also, as noted in Chapter 2, tried in 1950 to intervene directly in the Cold War with his 10-point peace plan. Much of it actually urged UN members to live up to their commitments in the UN Charter, but other aspects were aimed at diminishing the tension of the Cold War. As it was largely ignored and then overshadowed by the invasion of South Korea by the regime in the North, it probably remained only as a warning that the member governments did not necessarily welcome advice on major political issues from the Secretary-General.

When Great Britain turned the shards of its League of Nations mandate in Palestine over to the United Nations in 1947, Lie and the organization had to face not only the beginning of dissolution of old imperial systems, underway in the British colony of India, but also growing disorder and an imminent war in the Middle East. The route chosen by both the General Assembly and the Security Council during the 1948 war that led to the creation of the state of Israel was that of pacific settlement of the dispute. Lie energetically took part in the appointment and support of the field mission that suffered the assassination of the first UN representative, Folke Bernadotte, and carried on to the armistice negotiated by Ralph Bunche. The latter, who was the Secretariat specialist on the colonial world, had been dispatched by Lie as the chief UN Secretariat aide to Bernadotte. The Palestine negotiations also established field observation and structures for conciliation that provided experience for later peace-keeping missions. This set of incidents and responses, as well as a few others of lesser impact, helped open the way for the Secretary-General to figure in pacific settlement of disputes. Over the years, his role grew and often had public dimensions.

Hammarskjöld mostly avoided public campaigns and initiatives in favor of what he called "quiet diplomacy" and "preventive diplomacy" which took place outside public view. Yet some of his diplomatic efforts became highly public, as in the case of the negotiation to free the American airmen imprisoned by China during the Korean war. Moreover, he unmistakably challenged United States policy with regard to the elections in Lebanon in 1958, when a UN observation mission overlapped with the use of American troops in the region.[2]

More typical of his policy initiatives, however, were those in the case of the first peacekeeping expedition and the creation of the massive UN program after the breakdown of government in the Congo in 1960. In these instances, Hammarskjöld undertook no campaign to change the policies of the Cold Warriors but rather found space for a UN role between their positions. He worked assiduously, too, to ensure the concurrence of the Security Council and also in the case of the Congo rather quickly and spectacularly lost Soviet support.

Like Lie and later Secretaries-General, Hammarskjöld clearly was formulating precedents for the scope of his office. But his approach was less that of a participating politician than of a senior civil servant with specialized knowledge and skills to advise ministers and supervise the application of what had been decided. He used the acceptance of his initiatives to formulate a doctrine, as he did with quiet and preventive diplomacy, based on legal capacities stated or implied in the UN Charter. This he typically did either by a speech at a university[3] or some other reputedly neutral venue, or in a bland report to the Security Council or General Assembly, summing up the principles of a recent experience. Moreover, like his predecessor, he did not hesitate to defend his position when directly challenged by a government representative. He did so in a dramatic fashion in the General Assembly when the Soviet leader, Nikita Khrushchev, mercilessly denounced him there and in effect proposed abolishing the office and replacing it with a *troika*.

The first two Secretaries-General doubtless felt some urgency in establishing precedents for their office. Certainly Lie as the occupant of a new office in a new organization at a time of considerable optimism about its potential acted to create firm foundations. As his speeches made clear, Hammarskjöld had explicit ideas about his role as an impartial servant of the UN Charter. His sometimes imaginative probing for room for action between the Cold War protagonists was also followed by explicit claims that his actions belonged both to his office and the spirit of the UN Charter. It is noteworthy, too, that both Lie and Hammarskjöld eventually encountered crippling opposition from the Soviet Union at a time when it and its few allies were left isolated in the Security Council and outvoted in the General Assembly.

Despite the inhibitions of the Cold War, by the time that U Thant replaced Hammarskjöld, some fairly clear openings for initiatives by the Secretary-General had been found. When the Security Council or the General Assembly approved a response to a challenge that required carrying out a program, the Secretary-General became a key participant. His advice about the capacity of the Secretariat and the nature of the tasks to be carried out had some – often important – effects on both the mandate that he was given and the organization of the responses to it.

Thus, the Secretary-General appointed the senior officials to head the missions, his staff in New York had oversight over them, and he reported to the appropriate UN organs. But all of this depended on whether the Cold War protagonists saw either possible advantages in UN involvement and wanted to avoid more confrontation or else were so indifferent to the issue that they were content for it to remain an obscure affair to which the Secretary-General could apply quiet diplomacy.

The middle trio, 1953–1991

After Hammarskjöld, the next three Secretaries-General all had to work within the limits set by the Cold War. They had to bear in mind the dampening result for their office of openly colliding with policies that a permanent member of the Security Council intended relentlessly to promote. If the Soviet Union appeared especially opposed to an enlarged role for the Secretary-General and his organization in Cold War issues, after the election of General Dwight Eisenhower as president of the United States in 1952, its government also reduced earlier American willingness to shape its policies in the UN crucible. Thus Thant, Waldheim and Pérez de Cuéllar – the middle Trio – usually had perhaps even less room in which to maneuver than their predecessors.

Partly the political fate imposed by the Soviet Union on Lie and Hammarskjöld invited caution; so did the passing of the excitement of founding a unique institution. None of the Trio produced either broad manifestos to which governments were urged to adhere or pioneering politico-administrative innovations. Yet all of them, in one way or another, usually associated with decisions by other organs or with continuing concerns, made suggestions for improving or applying broad policies or took specific initiatives in conflicts.

Some themes continually got endorsement and support from the Secretaries-General of the Trio during a period when the membership of the organization grew continually. The increasing tempo of the process of decolonization was one of these themes. The first significant examples dated back to the beginning of the United Nations with the formation of Syria and Lebanon as independent states, followed by the British withdrawal from India and, almost at the same time, from Palestine. The British West African colony, the Gold Coast, became independent Ghana in 1957. From then on, the rush of state formation doubled and then tripled the UN membership. This process, most of it peaceful, was urged on and honored by the Secretaries-General.

Closely related to decolonization was the theme of economic development. If UN membership signaled the replacement of colonies by independent states, the unevenly distributed economic and social development increased in salience. The Secretaries-General during the Trio era passed up no chance to urge on cooperation among the members to support and advance programs of economic development.

Backed by distinguished economic analysis by members of the Secretariat, their chiefs also took part in the construction of improved or new mechanisms for promoting development. These included the UNDP, that concentrated on technical assistance, and UNCTAD with its ambitious approach to trade. An autonomous part of the Secretariat did the staff work for the negotiations required by the provisional organization around the General Agreement on Tariffs and Trade that substantially lowered barriers to free trade and eventually became the World Trade Organization outside the UN framework.

The remarkable series of special topical world conferences sponsored by the United Nations beginning in the 1970s offered the Secretaries-General chances to speak, if not necessarily closely to cooperate, with a broader public that went beyond conventional diplomacy. Their addresses to such gatherings offered the delegations base lines and suggestions from which to work. At the same time, little data can be found on which to estimate the effects of such appearances. Nevertheless, whatever prestige the Secretary-General personally may have brought to the gatherings added to the persuasiveness of the final declarations.

As always, issues of peace and security preoccupied the Secretaries-General of the Trio. None of them, however, attempted any initiatives as broadly conceived as Lie and Hammarskjöld had undertaken on their own. Rather, they worked with ameliorative or adjusting intentions within the framework of existing missions or around their edges. They continued and kept alive Hammarskjöld's notions of quiet and preventive diplomacy. In a sense, such conserving practices could be understood as the normal, precedent-based behavior of a senior organizational executive. From another point of view, even within approved programs mounted by the Security Council, any initiative might prove controversial and thus bring little credit to the Secretary-General.

Examples of such narrow initiatives have abounded throughout the history of the United Nations. During the Trio period, as noted earlier, Thant decided to withdraw the peace-keeping contingent from the Suez region after Israel and the Arab neighbors renewed their hostilities in 1956. Particularly in the United States, parts of the government and of public opinion viewed this as deliberately hostile to Israel. Thant also worked with Adlai Stevenson, then head of the US Mission to the UN, in a secret attempt to start direct negotiations between Washington and North Vietnam.[4] This attempt was long discretely shielded from public view, but its failure led Thant in speeches fruitlessly to appeal to the United States to end its war in Vietnam.

Examples of more successful initiatives were the open diplomatic campaigns by Pérez de Cuéllar, who had the backing of the Security Council in using representatives in the serious conflicts in Central America and in Afghanistan. In both instances, the Secretary-General's personal representatives negotiated understandings with the parties to the conflicts that were followed with formal conferences to promote further progress.[5] The conference on Afghanistan in April 1998, reported Pérez de Cuéllar, was "the first instance of the world's two most powerful States [the USA and the Soviet Union] becoming the co-guarantors of an agreement negotiated under the auspices of the Secretary-General".[6] It became obvious in retrospect that the war in Afghanistan strongly contributed to the end of the Cold War. In addition to organizing a good offices mission to deal with the left-over issues with Pakistan, the Secretary-General posted a Coordinator to Afghanistan to help with reconstruction.

If the involvement of the Secretary-General in the aftermath of the Soviet withdrawal from Afghanistan marked a loosening of the United Nations from the anchors of the Cold War, the response of the Security Council to the invasion of Kuwait by Iraq led many observers at the time to the conclusion that at last the collective security idea of the UN Charter had been applied. At the end of his term, Pérez de Cuéllar hailed it "a great turning point in history" and pointed to "the renaissance of the Organization".[7]

Increasing post-Cold-War activism

Boutros-Ghali took office in the optimistic glow of the success of the Security Council in presiding over the successful enforcement action in expelling the Iraqi invaders from Kuwait. Not only did the force headed by the United States quickly defeat the Iraqi invaders, but the Security Council also created controls to limit Iraqi military potentials. The moment seemed to some observers a triumph for international organization.

In the realm of advancing policy, the Security Council met in 1992, early in Boutros-Ghali's term, at the level of heads of government and directed him to advise it on improving UN peace-preserving functions. "I had been asked to assume more responsibility than any of my predecessors" was his hyperbolic reaction.[8]

Boutros-Ghali seized the opportunity for initiative with enthusiasm. It resulted in a report to the Security Council entitled "Agenda for Peace".[9] Among its several recommendations, most of them in fact underpinned by the implicit hope that UN members would at last do what they had pledged in the UN Charter, were proposals for a rapid response military force and preventive intervention in developing challenges to peace as well as many technical provisions. Even if the optimistic atmosphere encouraged him, the Secretary-General obviously tried with this document to initiate broad policy changes among many governments, including the weighty Permanent Five. He moreover followed it with another "Agenda", this one for economic and social cooperation[10] and an update on the security document.

The optimism that impelled these requested initiatives soon vanished, however, under the impetus of the Somalia debacle and the beginning of the long, at first floundering, attempt on the part of the Security Council and other international bodies to cope with the results of the dissolution of Yugoslavia. Here, too, Boutros-Ghali made suggestions and offers of help and used his staff in the process, but the atmosphere proved too corrosive and confused for even mild leadership from his office. Under merciless pressure from the United States, as noted in Chapter 3, his one term ended in bitterness and little outcome from his policy initiatives.

Yet Boutros-Ghali's activism left behind examples for his successor both to use and avoid. In general, Kofi Annan had precedents for using assemblies of high-ranking national political leaders as thresholds for active engagement in policy issues. He also could learn from the record of more than a half century in his office, if his experience in the Secretariat had not already made it clear, that tactful approaches and the building of support among governments constituted necessary foundations for initiatives.

Twenty-first century

By the opening of the new century and after more than 50 years of UN experience, the organization and its chief administrative officer, for good or ill, unquestionably were part of the international system. Both the United Nations and international relations had nuances that in 1945 would have seemed improbable. One of these, it could inferred from the tone that the Secretaries-General gave their initiatives, was a broadening beyond diplomatic networks of participants in UN decisions and programs. By the time that Annan had settled into the office and had won a second appointment ahead of schedule, both the nature of such initiatives and their targets appeared to reflect these changes.

No Secretary-General could, of course, neglect the diplomatic circuit which is inevitably a primary target of initiatives in an organization of states. And none did. In some ways, the diplomatic public grew more complex over the years as the membership of the organization more than tripled. Moreover, some of the large new members, such as Nigeria, were formidable factors in a multilateral organization. In other important states, such as China, the Soviet Union, Iran, Brazil and Argentina, the orientation of government policy had sharply turned. Beyond that, other modes of international organization evolved. These included, among others, the NAM, the Group of 77, the European Union, the Conference of Islamic States, and the summit meetings of the leading industrial countries. In addition, as Annan settled into office, the United Nations had in Yugoslavia entered into relations with NATO that would have been unthinkable during the Cold War.

Beyond the tangle of cooperation with an increasing number of governments and the basket of other international organizations, active elements of civil society also formed a growing public. When Annan was appointed, civil society was represented if only in a fragmented way by NGOs with various aims, especially those promoting human rights, development and humanitarian relief. Indeed, over the years, some of them or their services had become virtually a part of the UN institutions.

One venerable attention-getting opportunity that all of the Secretaries-General used with various degrees of enthusiasm had its base in proclamations of special days, weeks, months, years and even decades devoted to specific topics. From the beginning, UN practice marked the date of adoption of the UN Charter. A Human Rights Day soon followed. By the 1960s, the General Assembly added to the growing list the first Decade of Development, which inevitably was followed by a second and third. The Secretary-General unfailingly had messages or speeches for these occasions as heads of governments and ministers in national governments do. Such communications help maintain contact with client groups and, in the case of governments, are a standard feature of diplomatic protocol.

The penultimate year of Boutros-Ghali's term coincided with the fiftieth anniversary of the organization. Part of the General Assembly session that year was turned into a grand ceremony with 127 heads of state or government in attendance. Much special notice was generated by the presence of Pope John Paul II who addressed the gathering. President Clinton, whose diplomats were increasingly at odds with Boutros-Ghali, praised the blushing Secretary-General for his leadership at a troubled moment when no less than 70,000 UN peacekeepers were at their stations.[11] Nevertheless, little of substance emerged from a strenuous organizational effort, although much momentary publicity came out of the session. The next year saw Boutros-Ghali under personal attack in the American presidential campaign and his organization the subject of controversy tinged with contempt.

Yet the fiftieth anniversary fitted the notion that the publics attuned to the United Nations had broadened. Conventional diplomatic practice would hardly have demanded or obtained the presence of so many political dignitaries for a symbolic gathering. The UN engagement in peacekeeping, promotion of economic development, environmental protection and human rights, as well as growing humanitarian relief, sets a heavy agenda for diplomats and UN organs. But these were subjects that summit gatherings treat only as broad policy in speeches and final exhortatory declarations that customarily were a mile wide and an inch deep. As much as anything else, the fiftieth anniversary session was pointed at broad publics that were never directly represented in UN activity or expected as participants.

Annan has addressed major initiatives to publics that included, but went well beyond, familiar diplomatic proceedings in UN deliberative organs. In his first report to the General Assembly, he showed his awareness of these broader publics in underlining globalization and civic society as factors underlying the agenda.[12] By 1998, he and his staff were preparing for the new century as a symbol of change and for a Millennium Assembly that would was go far beyond earlier ceremonial meetings, such as that for the fiftieth anniversary. He gave notice of an intention to develop a major policy initiative that lives on as the

"Millennium Goals".[13] These were accompanied by a monitoring mechanism that included the entire UN system and additional reporting.

Following trends in official participation in UN-summoned summits, the Millennium Assembly in September 2000 brought together more senior national representatives than ever before – the "mother of all conferences" said the wags – and will not likely be succeeded by anything more inclusive or ambitious. Altogether, 147 heads of state or governments attended. They adopted, as is customary, a declaration of desirable policies, although mass media concentrated on the heads of major governments. These were the undertakings that would be monitored. The unanimously approved document began with identifying key values, some of which represented the evolution of the ideas of 1945 underlying the UN Charter:

- Freedom.
- Equality
- Solidarity
- Tolerance
- Respect for nature
- Shared responsibility

This was followed by specific undertakings listed under eight headings:

- Peace, security and disarmament
- Development and poverty eradication
- Protecting our common environment
- Human rights, democracy and good governance
- Protecting the vulnerable
- Meeting the special needs of Africa
- Strengthening the United Nations

Annan's seminal policy document, "We the peoples: the role of the United Nations in the twenty-first century",[14] set out views that gave form to his subsequent public initiatives. Globalization, he pointed out, had contributed to fundamental change in international relations. The UN decision-making structures did not conform to contemporary needs of governance (not governing). "Better governance means greater participation, coupled with accountability. Therefore, the international public domain – including the United Nations – must be opened up further ... Depending on the issues at hand, this may include civil society organizations, the private sector, parliamentarians, local authorities, scientific associations, educational institutions and many others."[15]

These recent broadening approaches to promote UN policy and Annan's own notions about it had wide, if sometimes skeptical, acceptance. They trod the delicate tightrope between policy leadership and anonymous service of the classical staff function. They were directed not exclusively to the usual public of national representatives engaged in negotiation on recommendations proposed in UN deliberative organs. They more strongly than ever before implied his reaching across national boundaries to publics that ultimately had political

The Secretary-General's travels in the summer of 2004

June 9-10: Cambridge, MA, Honorary degree at Harvard University.

June 11: Washington, DC, President Reagan's funeral.

June 12-15: Brazil, UNCTAD session and senior Brazilian leaders.

June 28-29: United Arab Emirates, official visit.

June 29-30: Qatar, official visit.

June 30-July 3: Sudan and Chad, re Darfur humanitarian crisis.

July 3: Eritrea, official visit and UN peace-keeping mission.

July 3-7: Ethiopia, address to African Union session, meetings with senior African leaders.

July 7-8: Kenya, situation in Sudan and Somalia and UN agencies in Nairobi.

July 9- 13: Thailand, opened International AIDS Conference and met senior regional leaders.

July 14-17: Austria, met UN High Level Panel on Threats, Challenges, and Change and head of UN mission in Kosovo and Austrian and other officials.

July 27-31: Ghana, situation of UN mission in Ivory Coast and Ivorian and Ghanaian presidents.

August Vacation.

August 18-19: Switzerland, commemoration of anniversary of bombing of UN office in Baghdad. Met senior officials.

September 7-9: Mexico, official visit. Met President Fox and senior leaders.

September 10: New York, General Assembly begins later in the month.

(UN Press Releases SG/T/2407-2420).

persuasiveness. They necessarily pointed to actions by state apparatuses, more than the private sector, for executing programs.

Even if national leaders who approved strong state involvement in social issues backed such initiatives, not all the proposed partners beyond the diplomatic publics reacted with enthusiasm or without suspicion. Although the Global Compact had enlisted substantial global corporations, most so far abstained. Among NGOs, some avoided any official connections while others had views that opposed the recommendations of the Secretary-General and the General Assembly. The latter included activists who had begun in the 1990s to disturb meetings of international organs. Finally, no one really knew how far the messages of initiatives would eventually carry.

UN public information

A substantial part of the UN Secretariat is explicitly devoted to spreading the messages inherent in decisions and programs of the organization, including the thoughts of the Secretary-General. This activity is centered in the Department of Public Information (DPI), headed by an Under-Secretary-General. It has a staff of just under 750 and expends some 19 percent of the regular budget.[16]

For many journalists, whose media only occasionally give attention to UN affairs, DPI is a ready source of facts, statements by officials and full transcripts of what the Secretary-General has said in public. At the same time, most of what UN organs officially do is open to all comers, including journalists, academic researchers and representatives of NGOs, for whom access is made easy. Although media coverage of the General Assembly over the years fell to such a low level that the representatives there urged the DPI to do more to encourage attention,[17] anyone who wishes can in person follow all of its plenary sessions and its main committees and can obtain press releases covering most of what is in progress or done.

For active media representatives, DPI provides the services of an official spokesperson and staff who can be consulted at almost any time. Yet access and availability of information obviously does not add up to a universally well-informed public or even perhaps to minimal understanding of complex procedure, programs and responsibilities.

Both the mandate and operations of DPI have been subject to continuous criticism and as well as support.[18] The basic mandate, pronounced by the General Assembly in 1946,[19] directed it to promote among the peoples of the world an informed understanding of UN work and purposes. But it was also always pointed towards helping communications media with impartial information and filling in gaps rather than serving as the principal source or distribution channel. The task has been complicated by the existence of monopolistic state media, censorship and very uneven development of publications and electronic media. At times, some media voices claimed that DPI competed with their services. Yet a majority of the General Assembly always treated DPI, if expensive, as necessary.

By 2002, DPI had had gone through seven periodic reviews by UN decisional organs and one major restructuring.[20] It underwent an annual examination by a specialized committee of the General Assembly as well as consideration by an advisory body. With a new head in 2002, DPI once more undertook a review which accorded with the general reorganizing initiative undertaken by Annan. It resulted in a "clear mission statement" that DPI "is to help fulfill the substantive purposes of the United Nations by strategically communicating the activities and concerns of the Organization to achieve the greatest public impact".[21] Important structural reforms of the department also were undertaken, including shrinking the network of more than 70 information centers to a hub system serving several surrounding lands. This, too, brought challenges from some governments that were anxious for whatever reason, among which were financial, to continue to host the existing centers.

The routine production of DPI consists of material and services directed both to media that bring the contents to their audiences and other means of reaching out to publics through its own facilities. It issues press releases on all open meetings of the General Assembly and the Security Council; organizes press conferences for the Secretary-General; provides a daily briefing in New York for correspondents; films the proceedings of many meetings and records speeches and other statements which are then available to media; and constantly augments with its own pictures a photographic library, also available to media. Some of this material is sent to the information centers for redistribution. DPI also is responsible for the UN libraries in New York and Geneva, which serve media, delegation members and the Secretariat.

The attempts to reach broader audiences include production of films and radio programs, and particular themes as well as news. UN radio is reported to broadcast live and by tape to 140 radio stations in 75 countries and claims to reach 130 million listeners in seven languages.[22] It produces a weekly TV show available to broadcasters. It publishes the *Yearbook of the United Nations* which is written by DPI staff. Beyond that are brochures and books on UN topics and mounting the tours of thousands of visitors to the New York headquarters.

All of these services use the initiatives of the Secretary-General, his words and his emphases as convenient focal points. Even the *Yearbook,* perhaps the slowest of the media, now contains the text of the Secretary-General's annual report on the work of the organization, as well as a signed foreword.

During the last decade, DPI has complemented its older services and used their output to feed an active site on the Internet that is open to all. (The URL is: http://www.un.org.) It provides documentation that was once only available in libraries, the texts of the Secretary-General's statements, news services, links to other parts of the UN system, and much more.

While such facilities obviously open wider access to UN proceedings, accomplishments and frustrations, their impact – what is sought by all "information services" – remains uncertain. DPI has little facility for systematic research on the effects of its messages and access points. The prospective consumers of such information not only need access to the transmissions and Internet sites but also have to be able to take in the conceptual underpinnings of multilateral organizations. Listeners to radio news and television viewers in the last decade would perhaps be impressed with the frequency that the Secretary-General's words and images appear, but their responses clearly are not at the order of DPI.

Even in information-inundated America the outcome of the flood of news coverage and information in crucial debates raises skepticism.[23] At the same time, opinion surveys have continually shown a high level of approval for the United Nations as such, although on specific actions the results are mixed.[24]

7   Conclusion

The victors of World War II had every reason to entertain grandiose thoughts when they designed the United Nations. In the closing phase of the war, they sought a less violent world than they had just experienced. It would develop the best cooperative characteristics of a supreme alliance, such as that of the victors in World War II, and so overwhelmingly repel force. UN members would accept legal obligations to pay close attention to the needs and rights of individual persons. The enemy that they had defeated represented at the time a lawless opposite of the UN aims. It seemed the fleeting moment to take advantage of victory.

In the improved universe implied by the UN Charter, an international official and his staff would not exert authority over states that remain the basis of international relations. But on occasion international officials might convince them of conduct that would fulfill the aims to which they had subscribed. The Secretary-General could hardly cherish utopian notions. The new international mechanisms looked to resolving the most refractory issues of world politics: pacific settlements of disputes that could lead to war; improving the welfare of people everywhere; protecting their rights; promoting self-government of colonial possessions; and more. This agenda would obviously not yield to instantaneous remedies. The Secretary-General could, however, strive in a practical manner to assist the organization resolve such issues. In other words, the United Nations was designed with the expectation that it could help with emergencies and could hack away at the underbrush of long-term global problems.

Even if the United Nations has not become the central point of international relations for all governments on every issue, the Secretary-General and his Secretariat, as expected, have developed into a much-used instrument of the organization. In the course of that development, the UN Charter has been proved a flexible constitution, rather than merely a limiting law, while both the organization and the office of Secretary-General have survived and, it could be argued, grown more persuasive through the Cold War. The Secretary-General occasionally could initiate or significantly help shape global policy. On their own, the Secretariat and the Secretary-General could indeed carry out the combined wishes of the member governments on some important issues. They, then, are an integral factor in international politics.

How big a factor? Firm generalizations seem well-nigh impossible. The office has inherent limitations. It calls for a direct participant in policy making – a Secretary-General with protected international status who nevertheless remains responsible to, and serves, the same intergovernmental councils that, usually with some contribution from him or his staff, take final decisions. This is a formula for treating issues in their context, for negotiating in a diplomatic style and for possible confusion as to responsibility.

In the "high politics" of peace and security, the constraints on the Secretary-General were soon always visible. Although he has been allowed or asked to furnish analytical advice to the Security Council, he never has had the staff facilities, the diplomatic networks, the intelligence services of governments even in the second or third power rank. Nor did pleas for better arrangements get much sympathy from governments that masked their suspicion of international organization with claims of sanctity or their own financial penury. Even when the Security Council mandated field missions operated with military personnel, the Secretary-General had only the slenderest staff for military advice. Yet he at times was responsible for the operations of tens of thousands of troops borrowed from many commands and scattered around the world in trouble spots.

Nevertheless, the Security Council and the General Assembly, after getting the advice of the Secretary-General on costs and financing of field missions, in recent times often decided to initiate more or to expand them. That often posed financial as well as organizational difficulties. And it was left to the Secretary-General to persuade usually reluctant governments to make available the necessary personnel and to forward promised replenishments of the treasury.

The Secretary-General had no role in directing the large-scale enforcement actions in Korea and Iraq under Chapter 7 of the UN Charter. But as he serves the Security Council in the course of its business, he could follow the results of decisions. Whether he could succeed in shaping such campaigns so as to make post-war reconstruction and humanitarian relief more efficient seems doubtful.

In cases of expanded peacekeeping, as in Cambodia, Somalia and former Yugoslavia, the Secretary-General's role also enlarged. His representatives in the field had duties and opportunities that substantially affected the immediate operations. The senior officials of the Secretariat acquired new experience and, some hoped, additional capabilities.

As the spread of highly destructive, cheap weapons to troubled areas of the world made possible heavy attacks on civilians, and smoldering ethnic frictions were enflamed, unanticipated humanitarian needs accompanied peace-maintenance. Here, too, the operation of the Secretary-General and the Secretariat as a warning and coordinating mechanism took on increasing proportions. Especially during Annan's second term, his public reactions made it obvious that the Secretary-General and his staff closely tracked events. They used information from the field missions to underpin instructions and strove to expand their persuasiveness on both the military-related aspects of disturbances to the peace and the accompanying humanitarian needs.

Beyond peace and security, the UN agenda always is wide, long and exceedingly complex. For the most part, the Secretary-General himself has not been a participant in detailed decisions on economic and social cooperation. He acts rather as a top-level generalist whose stated opinions are backed by Secretariat expertness. Indeed, the unrelenting demands on the Secretary-General in matters of peace-maintenance raise the question of how he might have time for anything else. At the same time, the diplomatic background of most of the Secretaries-General, along with the immediate agendas of the Permanent Five, doubtless inclined them towards primary attention to the peace-maintenance function.

Early in the twenty-first century, there was no sign that the Secretary-General had diminished attention to the peace and security matters. Annan's willingness – perhaps eagerness – to send senior officials to violent situations and to share his views of political developments with mass media suggested ever more active surveillance. Moreover, he appeared to be fully informed and often a participant in confidential discussions among the Permanent Five of the Security Council. Some of his statements dealt with insurrections, ethnic conflicts and internal disturbances with member states. These would once have set off diplomatic rows but seemingly have been tolerated.

Annan missed few opportunities to urge his organization to greater efforts in humanitarian disasters, the campaign against AIDS and pacification and development in Africa. His messages to a long list of international gatherings on subjects ranging from global warming to individual human rights made clear that at least the rhetorical scope of his office had been much expanded as compared with the early years or, before them, the League of Nations.

In part, Annan's tenure witnessed a continuation at a stiffer pace of concerns that had appeared earlier. The earlier attention to disasters as well as to human rights distantly suggested that the United Nations had a vaguely defined relationship with civil society. This relationship grew with the institutionalization of NGOs in global conferences organized by the United Nations. It was rhetorically embraced by the Trio and by Boutros-Ghali. It was farther extended by Annan with the endorsement by the General Assembly of the Millennium Goals, his approach to the private sector with the Global Compact and the interest of private philanthropists in supporting the UN programs to cope with AIDS and malaria.

All of this approach to the relationships with parts of civic society, including access by individuals to UN official records and other publications, was made much more direct by the development of electronic communications. The UN Secretariat had by the first years of the twenty-first century energetically promoted their use for emitting messages, serving a broader public and keeping track of developments.

Managing the Secretariat

As head of the Secretariat, the Secretary-General has tasks that constantly undergo revision. Whatever his plans and the suggestions of his staff, the Secretary-General has to look to the General Assembly for final approval on such important matters as staff rules, adoption of the budget, financing and even acquiescence of his senior appointments.

The General Assembly, where the criticism of management is voiced by governments, has almost unceasingly pressed for what its members understand as efficiency and economy. At the same time, it and the Security Council have continuously added to the UN agenda while financial contributions have rarely kept pace. Ideas emanating from the Secretariat for the improvement of services or for new projects also add to the agenda. Some of the expansions or changes suggested by the Secretariat came, of course, at the bidding of other organs, but others resulted from efforts of UN personnel to improve services.

Precisely what efficiency and economy mean in the context of the UN Secretariat remains unclear, as generally carrying out programs depends on the apparatuses of the member states. That greatly complicates precise measurement. Nevertheless, in the name of efficiency and economy, the General Assembly has repeatedly called on the Secretary-General to limit the budget. On taking office, he has usually somewhat shifted the elements of the Secretariat to suit his personal style. In response to the calls from the General Assembly, usually led by the principal donor governments, to economize, the Secretary-General has repeatedly reorganized the Secretariat, in some cases reducing the number of staff members even while adding departments. He has also changed the methodology of the budget and its documentation. None of these gestures has ever fully satisfied all of the UN members. Nor have they prevented the development of recurring financial crises.

While some governments press for more expensive or additional programs as their own delegates vote for "economy" measures, the General Assembly has augmented its devices for overseeing the budget process. This has obviously affected the discretionary area of the Secretary-General and thus in fact cut back on the exercise of his responsibility. Whether the elaborate mechanism has increased efficiency remains unclear.

In personnel management, too, the formal provisions both add to the duties of the Secretary-General and his staff and diminish the discretion to carry them out. The General Assembly has approached the character of the international civil service, the protection of which is a legal obligation of members and of the Secretary-General, by in fact setting the geographical distribution requirement above the competence of appointees. Viewed through the cloudy lenses of efficiency and economy, it is possible to make a strong argument that nothing is gained by such practices. But examined as political fact, they fit with the primacy of the member states in international organization.

Whether a truly international service, as called for by the UN Charter, could ever exist, still remains an unsettled question and an unchanged formal goal. Much clearer, however, is the fact that a succession of leading Secretariat members have acted in an impartial manner and gained widespread praise and recognition for it. When they have come under pressure because of their independence, their chief usually, but not invariably, has defended them. But he too has felt heavy pressure from member governments, including the use or threat of the veto at times of his possible reappointment.

By now, especially in maintaining peace and security, the Secretary-General is an accepted partner as well as servant of the Security Council. Moreover, with the Secretariat, he has become a presence, if sometimes distant, in trying to cope with a long list of international issues. Nevertheless, the history of some six decades leaves little doubt that on occasion his help, offered or requested, can be brushed aside by the member countries, especially the richest and strongest.

Personal attributes

Inevitably the "personality" of the Secretary-General has attracted comment. While the vagueness of the term matches some of the specula-tion about its effects, interest in "personality" does call attention to a person in a public position. In part, that attention derives from the Secretary-General as a senior entry on diplomatic protocol lists: he is often seen in the company of heads of government and state. His visibility makes him something of a celebrity. The nature of some of his work, too, brings him attention: he receives mandates connected with wars, notorious violations of human rights and handling of major global issues. That leaves the question as to whether his personal attributes – a less loaded term than "personality" – make much difference and, if so, to whom.

Taken together, the Secretaries-General and the Secretariat obviously constitute a polyglot band acting in a universe that outclasses the tower of Babel for diversity. How the words and deeds of an individual inter-national servant come across in this universe clearly varies from one part to another and depends on translation, choice of metaphors and phrases, and even body language. Only one of them, Lie, had faced the challenge of the hustings where an unknown but live audience awaited words it could understand. No wonder then that the Secretaries-General usually have favored the bland language of diplomacy.

Some of the Secretaries-General – Hammarskjöld and Boutros-Ghali would be examples – have exuded intelligence. But even those two provide striking contrasts, partly because the 1950s of Hammarskjöld's term were not constantly observed by television cameras and mass media that leave no foible unrecorded. Hammarskjöld had close friend-ships with leading artists and writers. He translated a French poet, who had also been a senior foreign affairs official, and wrote a mystical self-examination that was published after his death.[1] Even though his discourse was underpinned by high culture, for a time, he managed good communications with what seemed a broad public. In that he took advantage of the interest of the mass media in the dramas of war and peace in which the Secretary-General then was a leading figure.

Annan operates in a different media era. Television and quick recording of speech, even what is said through a car window, has become routine. He has a calm rhetorical style and chooses his words with care so as not to offend governments directly even when he is crit-ical. His demeanor is confidently dignified but never strikes, at least to English-speakers, arrogant or self-serving notes. He is indeed ready to submit to the questions of the media representatives and treats them with respect. As it always had been with his predecessors, his own public relations corps always gives him special attention. He clearly uses good advice as to the moment to speak, the statements to publish and the interviews to grant. His speeches are polished but different and perhaps more personal in accent from those of Hammarskjöld.

Trygve Lie never seemed comfortable with the press and mass communications. But as the first in his office, he necessarily appeared often in the press and radio. Television was then less pervasive and still somewhat clumsy in recording events and had to depend primarily on using photographic film. That dictated dependence on scheduled, formal occasions in which personal attractiveness was at least partly overshadowed by protocol and deliberateness.

Lie's English and French pronunciation were strongly tinged with his native Norwegian tongue. His speeches and live appearances on film seemed ponderous. The photographic lens seemingly added more weight to his already robust figure and strong head. He had little of Hammarskjöld's wit and certainly none of his successor's connection to the art world.

Of all the Secretaries-General, perhaps Thant projected the least sharp public image. His use of English, long polished as a journalist and diplomat, was impeccable. But his style was always tempered and even retiring, perhaps the result of his cultural and religious background. His background included resistance to the British colonial regime in his native Burma, where he became one of the founders of the independent state. That gave him some ease with political engagement and a deep interest in decolonization. The latter was a subject of much interest to a large part of the world that still was colonial and had scanty mass communications. The messages sent by Thant about the colonial world, nevertheless, had less resonance in the parts that had the heaviest communication grids.

As the successor to Hammarskjöld, Thant could not, and arguably eschewed any attempt to, innovate policies of the magnitude of the responses to the Suez and Congo crises. The circumstance of his appointment gave him, as journalists at the time said, a "hard act to follow." His speeches lacked the intellectual quality of his predecessor and his interviews with the media, usually in English, were dampened by his modest manner. Nor did he succeed, or perhaps shunned, in building up much personal following in a broader public.

The two Secretaries-General who followed Thant had relatively standard diplomatic backgrounds. Waldheim came, like his predecessors, from a small country whose language had a relatively narrow following. He spoke English and fluent French with a German accent. Pérez de Cuéllar seemed more at home with French than English but could address the large number of Spanish speakers in his native language. Neither had much of a popular touch, although Waldheim tried harder than Pérez de Cuéllar to cultivate a public image as a zealous, innovative diplomat. Neither, however, had a remarkable degree of originality to communicate to a wider public.

Boutros-Ghali had a talent for sharp expression and wit that were hardly evident in his three predecessors. He clearly had important cultural and intellectual resources. His mastery of English and especially French were as obvious as his ambition to leave his mark. Yet his talents may not have served well in mass communications. The 14 votes he had in the Security Council for a second term that was vetoed by the United States nevertheless speak in favor of his diplomatic abilities.

Because only the top layer of the Secretariat owes its appointment directly to the Secretary-General and has contracts with limited terms of office, the majority of the staff stays in place when its chief is changed. As is standard in civil services, each new chief has to develop his own style of relationships with personnel whose appointment preceded his own. Here personal attributes might be expected to play a considerable role, but little basis aside from anecdotes exists for estimating how much and how deeply the person of the Secretary-General affected such relationships.

Obviously the immediate entourage of the Secretary-General radiates loyalty and respect. As to the other ranks, each Secretary-General has used the occasion of a Staff Day to address the entire Secretariat. On taking office, Hammarskjöld personally visited each office in New York and greeted each staff member. In other cases, most lower ranking staff members rarely came that close to their chief, although during his travels, he encounters more. Annan as a veteran of the Secretariat obviously had met many of those who became his subordinates when he took office. Boutros-Ghali had a reputation, judging by corridor comments, of keeping his distance from all but his immediate office. None of the Secretaries-General, as might be expected, could possibly have undertaken an "open door" policy whereby any staff member could consult him. At the same time, the cultural diversity of the Secretariat might stand in the way of personal tactics by the Secretary-General to promote feelings of closeness and comradeship with the staff.

Special position of the USA

From the conception of the United Nations to the present, the United States government has affected and sometimes dominated the fortunes of the Secretary-General and the Secretariat. Despite the strong

American basis for the United Nations as an organization with broad goals, its support has waxed and waned with each new president and each new crisis in international relations. The US Congress has always included members, sometimes a majority, whose skepticism of international commitments could turn UN decisions into domestic issues. As a result, the United States government has often approached such global issues as protection of human rights, assistance to governments for economic development and preserving the natural environment with reservations, hesitation and outright opposition. In matters of peace-maintenance, especially in the Middle East and during the Cold War, it has generally preferred close alliances to broad-based international discussion. As a permanent member of the Security Council and since World War II the single most powerful state in the world – some said a "hegemon" – it could block UN action where it wished and support what it would outside the global institution.

Inescapably, the Secretary-General has had to pay attention to the twists and turns in American policy. The degree of support from Washington could negate or ensure the success of his initiatives. Lack of support from the US Congress, especially if it were encouraged by the White House, could threaten the Secretariat with bankruptcy. Strong backing, as Hammarskjöld and Annan at times had from Washington on some issues, could help the prestige of the organization and its chief officer.

All of the Secretaries-General have maintained close contact with the US Mission of the United Nations. Conversations with the ambassador in New York often were complemented with telephone calls or personal visits to the Secretary of State and the President of the United States. Sometimes the Secretary-General had the opportunity for discussions with members of Congress, and Annan notably cultivated such contacts. The Department of Public Information early on set up an information office in Washington that gingerly built up contacts in a global news center.

Yet such relationships include perils. The Secretary-General cannot afford to appear to have lost his independence to American influence. Especially during the Cold War, he kept some distance from Washington as from Moscow. Some of the other UN members still on occasion take every opportunity to point out what they think is overweening American influence on the Secretary-General.

No matter how well-known and respected or popular personally a Secretary-General may be in the United States, he cannot appear to exceed the normal restraints that limit diplomats in their relationships with host governments. Taking partisan positions or linking too closely with supporters or opponents of a policy endorsed by the White House would quickly bring Washington's thunder and lightning to the head of the Secretary-General. Moreover, while the United Nations appears to have broad support in American opinion, on specific issues it falls away. Even helping to cope with the mundane frictions that grow out of activities of the large number of diplomats manning the offices maintained by UN member governments in New York can cause political storms. These neighborhood incidents – around for example parking privileges – can soon turn into gales of criticism and local opposition.

The United States maintains a large permanent delegation to the United Nations, headed by an ambassador who has been approved by the US Senate, as well as others of high rank. Most of its mission heads have had prominent political careers, although from time to time a professional diplomat has been appointed. From the beginning, the United States government has ranked the head of the delegation to the United Nations as a very senior ambassador. The mission has the reputation of keeping fully informed of the details of operations within the Secretariat. Senior members of the US Mission represent the United States in all of the UN organs. Reports from the delegation in New York, as well as smaller ones in Geneva and Vienna, flow to the Department of State. Instructions to the missions are supposed to emanate from there. These arrangements add up to a high capacity to form and put forward a position that has its basis not only in UN activities but also in the inherent power and domestic politics of the United States.

Whether the United States has fully accepted the notion of an international civil service is open to doubt. A continuing stream of opinion in the Congress opposes giving what it regards as special privileges to American nationals, such a diplomatic immunity while on UN business. This stream has broadened at times to make sure that financial contributions to the United Nations include accounting for the precise use of American funds. It has also resulted in Congressional decisions that reduced the United Nations to the verge of bankruptcy. This obviously has impaired the authority of the Secretary-General. Similarly, the United States for many years closely monitored appointments to the Secretariat, giving advice that would be costly to ignore.

Particularly during the Cold War, the opponents used questionable tactics to observe and affect the Secretariat. Some governments still do not hesitate to do so. If the United States then was not alone in diluting the protection of the Secretariat, its very prominence in the organization may have given what it did special effectiveness.

The future

Guessing what precisely may be ahead for the Secretary-General and the Secretariat may be compared to forecasting which apple will fall from a fruit-laden tree. Anything from the wing-beat of a wasp to an earthquake could break an apple stem from the branch. Likewise, in forecasting what would happen to the Secretary-General and Secretariat, the complexity of the UN system, the tasks assigned to the staff, the tangled mix of governmental policies in 191 states, the sheer accidental and the mixed reception of recommended global policies all leave a would-be prophet with either high abstraction or despair. About all that can be said with certainty is that the Secretary-General will always be obliged to deal with subject matter that involves political sensitivity on the one hand and unexpected but particular developments on the other.

That set of vague but fairly obvious generalizations does point to one probably accurate forecast: the prestige and persuasiveness of the Secretary-General and his staff will not be at the same level in the eyes of all governments at any one time. Different publics also will apply their own standards to judging the work of the chief UN officer. His handling of the overlapping issues of the UN agenda will always evoke varied responses as long as autonomous governments and a reasonably free flow of information exist. In short, the Secretary-General will face the usual political choices involved in trying to apply normative prescriptions to unknown developments that take place in an open future in a global realm.

If past patterns shape future outcomes, it seems likely that the relationship of the Secretary-General to serious crises will bring him most public attention and personal concern. As crises that build around military violence, deadly civil unrest, as well as epidemics and natural disasters have a dramatic quality, they will remain the focus of most media attention. Generally, this translates into news about a series of decisions by the Secretary-General, the Security Council and other UN bodies over a relatively short period. This attention tends to obscure other UN activity that has little discernible effects in the short term but may promise much for the more distant future.

The selection of the Secretary-General, built into the UN institutional calendar at the end of each five-year term of office, presages another important moment of choice. The incumbent can hope for another term, campaign for it, be denied any chance by one or more of the Permanent Five or withdraw from candidacy. No Secretary-General has served more than two terms. What governments will do when Annan's second term ends in 2006 is as unknown as his own choice.

Whenever a Secretary-General is to be appointed, journalistic chatter and corridor gossip almost always involves the topic of geographical distribution. The last Asian to be appointed was Thant. Since his time a Western European and a Latin American were selected. An Arabic-speaking African preceded Annan. Relying on the somewhat mystic principles of rotation and on the preference for nationals of lesser powers, the next Secretary-General would then have his roots in a small Asian land. In any case, a new occupant of the suite on the 38th floor of the UN headquarters building signifies at least some change in approaches to policy and to management of the Secretariat.

Whatever the verity of such speculation, the institutional arrangements of the United Nations mean that the Permanent Members of the Security Council will be engaged in the appointment of the Secretary-General. While they will not be heedless of the wishes of the rest of the members, their own estimates will come first. That means, too, that the United States government will have a leading, if not entirely dominant, role in the outcome.

As long as the United Nations exists – there is no immediate reason to suggest its disappearance – its chief administrative officer will have some role in the formation of global policies. As I hope this book makes clear, it can vary from weighty to negligible, more often than not depending on factors beyond the control of the Secretary-General. For some, he will offer hope for a peaceful, productive future. For others, he will stand for a powerless agency. His actions can add to or subtract from the influence of his choices but never change the essentially political nature of his office.

Notes

Foreword

1 Leon Gordenker, *The UN Secretary-General and the Maintenance of the Peace* (New York: Columbia University Press, 1967).
2 See Benjamin Rivlin and Leon Gordenker, eds., *The Challenging Role of the UN Secretary-General: Making "The Most Impossible Job in the World" Possible* (Westport, CO: Praeger, 1993).
3 Egon Ranshofen-Wertheimer, *The International Secretariat: A Great Experiment in International Administration* (Washington, DC: Carnegie Endowment for International Peace, 1945).

1 Introduction

1 See Ruth B. Russell, *A History of the United Nations Charter* (Washington: Brookings Institution, 1958) for an authoritative account of the Conference and its preparation.

2 Blueprint and evolution of an international office

1 For a stimulating treatment of these trends, see Craig N. Murphy, *International Organization and Industrial Change: Global Governance since 1850* (New York: Oxford University Press, 1994). For a close look at how multilateral assemblies are organized and work, see Johan Kaufmann, *Conference Diplomacy: an Introductory Analysis*, second revised edition (Dordrecht: Martinus Nijhoff Publishers, 1988).
2 The ILO, of which the United States was a member, is the only part of the League of Nations structure to survive World War II and to continue into our time as a UN Specialized Agency. The Universal Postal Union and what is now the International Telecommunications Union also survived the war and are now UN Specialized Agencies.
3 For a detailed account see Russell, *A History of the United Nations Charter.* Legal interpretations are explored in Bruno Simma (ed.), *The Charter of the United Nations: a commentary* (New York: Oxford University Press, 1994).

4 For details of how the League's Secretariat was conceived, see F.P. Walters, *A History of the League of Nations* (London: Oxford University Press, 1952), Chapter 7.

5 A brief discussion of this phase and the relevant source documents can be found in Leon Gordenker, *The UN Secretary-General and the Maintenance of Peace (*New York: Columbia University Press, 1967), 3–19. See also the study by a veteran of the League Secretariat, Egon F. Ranshofen-Wertheimer, *The International Secretariat* (Washington: Carnegie Endowment for International Peace, 1945).

6 The leadership of the first ILO Director-General, Albert Thomas, is described in Edward J. Phelan, *Yes and Albert Thomas,* (London: Cresset Press, 1949).

7 The UN Charter has the international legal status of a treaty. Each member that ratifies it signifies that it accepts the obligations set out in the document. It also provides in Article 103 that in case of a conflict between the Charter provisions and those of any other international agreement, the Charter shall prevail. In the United States, a treaty has the status of the supreme law of the land. See Article VI, US Constitution.

8 See Statute of the International Court of Justice, especially Articles 16, 17 and 19.

9 In contemporary American usage, he would now be designated as "chief executive officer".

10 Brian Urquhart and Erskine Childers, *A World in Need of Leadership: Tomorrow's United Nations* (Uppsala, Sweden: Dag Hammarskjöld Foundation, 1990)

11 For details on the first three appointments which posed lasting precedents, see Gordenker, *The UN Secretary-General and the Maintenance of Peace*, 34–63.

12 See his account. Trygve Lie, *In the Cause of Peace* (New York: Macmillan Co., 1954), Chapter XXII.

13 For an informed, politically sophisticated, biography, see Brian Urquhart, *Hammarskjöld* (New York: Harper & Row, 1972).

14 His memoir is U Thant, *View from the UN* (Newton Abbot, UK: David & Charles, 1977)

15 His memoir is Kurt Waldheim, *In the Eye of the Storm* (Bethesda, MD: Adler & Adler, 1986).

16 For his account of his selection, see Javier Pérez de Cuéllar, *Pilgrimage for Peace: a Secretary-General's Memoir* (New York: St. Martin's Press, 1997), 25–28.

17 His account is published as Boutros Boutros-Ghali, *Unvanquished* (New York: Random House, 1999).

18 See Lie, *In the Cause of Peace,* 45–49, and Simma, *The Charter of the United Nations*, 1085.

19 This advice was proferred by the UN Preparatory Commission that met in 1945 after the Charter was adopted. It met in London. See Gordenker, *The UN Secretary-General…,* 27–33 for brief account.

20 For fuller discussion, see Thomas G. Weiss, *International Bureaucracy* (Lexington, MA: D.C. Heath, 1975), and Norman A. Graham and Robert S. Jordan (eds), *The International Civil Service: Changing Roles and Concepts,* (New York, Pergamon Press, 1980).

3 The UN Secretariat and its responsible chief

1 See Jacques Fomerand, "UN Conferences: Media Events or Genuine Diplomacy", *Global Governance*, 2,3 (Sept.–Dec.1996), 361–76; and Michael G. Schechter, ed., *United Nations-sponsored World Conferences: Focus on Impact and Follow-up* (Tokyo: United Nations University Press, 2001).

2 See "Report of the Independent Inquiry into the actions of the United Nations during the 1999 genocide in Rwanda", UN Doc. S/1999/1257, 16 December 1999.

3 "Bureaucracy" has the neutral significance of a reasoned, continuing form of organization. It is not used here in a pejorative sense.

4 See Lie, *In the Cause of Peace,* Chap. 3.

5 Boutros Boutros-Ghali, *The Unvanquished,* 16.

6 A study by the US General Accounting Office found that in the biennium 1997–98, the General Assembly referred to 587 new tasks of which 20 percent had vague or open-ended mandates. US Congress, General Accounting Office, *United Nations: Reform Initiatives Have Strengthened Operations, but Overall Objectives Have Not Yet Been Achieved,* GAO/NS/AD-00–169, May 20, 2000, 13.

7 Formally the Under-Secretaries-General outrank the Assistant Secretaries-General, but in practice the latter have primarily technical assignments but may be regarded as part of the second level of officials.

8 Kurt Waldheim, *In the Eye of the Storm,* 45.

9 Goulding, *Peacemonger,* London, John Murray, 2002, 6. He remarks that he modeled his own tenure on that of Sir Brian Urquhart, his predecessor as head of peacekeeping and known as a leading example of independence from any one government.

10 A subject for piles of sensational journalism but very few documented cases or criminal trials. For a personal confession of espionage by a senior UN official of Soviet nationality, see Arkady N. Shevchenko, *Breaking with Moscow* (New York: Knopf, 1985).

11 Article 1 (3).

12 The Secretary-General reports annually on this topic under the title "Composition of the Secretariat", e.g. UN Doc. A/57/1414, 17 September 2002.

13 It is relevant both to his appointment and his career, to note that Bunche was a black American, an anthropologist who had done distinguished work in Africa and worked with Gunnar Myrdal on a path-breaking exploration of the importance of race in America, see Brian Urquhart, *Ralph Bunche – an American Life* (New York: W.W. Norton, 1993) and Benjamin Rivlin, ed., *Ralph Bunche – the Man and His Times* (New York: Holmes and Meier, 1990).

14 This largely ignored accomplishment is explored in Louis Emmerij, Richard Jolly and Thomas G. Weiss, *Ahead of the Curve? UN Ideas and Global Challenges,* (Bloomington, IN: Indiana University Press, 2001).

15 Goulding, who had been a British ambassador before joining the Secretariat, doubts that corruption in the UN service "is worse than in the public services of most member states", *Peacemonger*, 8. See also Yves Beigbeder, "Fraud, Corruption and United Nations Culture", in Dijkzeul

and Beigbeder, *Rethinking International Organizations: Pathology and Promise* (New York: Berghahn Books, 2003).

16 Unjustly, according to decisions of the UN Administrative Tribunal, an independent judicial organ which also adds an element of complexity to the management of personnel. Its judgment resulted in compensation which the US Government opposed to the dismissed persons.

17 See Urquhart, *Hammarokjöld,* 58–64.

18 "The Secretary-General and the UN Budget", in Rivlin and Gordenker, *The Challenging Role of the UN Secretary-General*, 98.

19 International Court of Justice, Advisory Opinions and Orders, Report 1962 (Advisory Opinion on Article 17, paragraph 2 of the Charter).

20 For a brief factual account, see Klaus Hufner, "Financing the United Nations: The Role of the United States", in Dijkzeul and Beigbeder, *Rethinking International Organization*, 29–53.

21 For the evolution of American political opinion and decisions on UN finances, see Edward C. Luck, *Mixed Messages: American Politics and International Organization 1919–1999* (Washington: Brookings Institution Press, 1999), 224–53.

22 It maintains an Internet site that offers continuing UN news and other information. See www.UNFoundation.org

23 See report of the Joint Inspection Unit, UN Doc. A/58/375, 17 September 2003.

4 The Secretary-General as world constable

1 See the Waldheim and Pérez de Cuéllar memoirs, cited earlier, for manifold examples.

2 Address at Oslo, 3 June 1958. See also Gordenker, *The UN Secretary-General* … , 159–60.

3 For a recent account, see Goulding, *Peacemonger.*

4 Ian Johnstone, "The Role of the UN Secretary-General, The Power of Persuasion Based on Law", *Global Governance*, 9, 4, Oct.–Dec. 2003, 441–58.

5 For a passionate eye-witness account, see Roméo Dallaire, *Shake Hands with the Devil: the failure of humanity in Rwanda* (Toronto: Random House Canada, 2003).

6 UN Doc. S/1999/1257, 16 December 1999, a report by an independent inquiry headed by former Swedish Prime Minister Ingvar Carlsson. For a well-informed, broader picture, see Susan L. Woodward, *Balkan Tragedy* (Washington: Brookings Institution, 1995).

7 "Statement on Receiving the Report of the Independent Inquiry on the Actions of the United Nations during the 1994 Genocide in Rwanda", United Nations, New York, 16 December 1999.

8 See Donald J. Puchala, "The Secretary-General and His Special Representatives", in Rivlin and Gordenker, *The Most Impossible Job* … , 81–97.

9 For a brief account, see UN Press Release SC/8113, 6 July 2004. It includes the complementary statement by the Secretary-General.

10 "Sudan: Envoy warns of ethnic cleansing as Security Council calls for ceasefire", UN News Service, www.UN.Org, 2 April 2004.

11 See his dramatic account in Kurt Waldheim, *In the Eye of the Storm,* Chapter 1.

12 See discussion in Leon Gordenker, *The UN Secretary-General ...* , 177–82, and Urquhart, *Hammarskjöld,* 129–31.

13 See Gordenker, *The United Nations and the Peaceful Unification of Korea: the Politics of Field Operations 1947–1950* (The Hague: Martinus Nijhoff, 1959).

14 Lie, *In the Cause of Peace,* 333–34.

15 Publications on peacekeeping in its manifold variations comprise a very large list. Some useful general studies are: Paul F. Diehl, *International Peacekeeping* (Baltimore: Johns Hopkins University Press, 1993); Alan James, *Peacekeeping in International Politics* (London: International Institute for Strategic Studies, 1990); and Olara A. Otunnu and Michael W. Doyle, eds, *Peacemaking and Peacekeeping for the New Century* (Lanham, MD: Rowman & Littlefield Publishers, 1998). For a set of comparative case studies with a military perspective, see John Mackinlay, *The Peacekeepers* (London: Unwin Hyman, 1989).

16 See Urquhart in *Hammarskjöld,* 159–230 for a detailed account of the diplomacy led by the Secretary-General.

17 For case studies of the observation missions and early peacekeeping, see William J. Durch, ed., *The Evolution of UN Peacekeeping* (New York: St. Martin's Press, 1993).

18 U Thant, *View from the UN, 220–52*, contains his detailed account of this incident.

19 See Urquhart, *Hammarskjöld,* Chapters 16–18, 21, and Thant, *View from the UN,* 95–153.

20 John Mackinlay and Jarat Chopra, "Second generation multinational operations", *Washington Quarterly* 15, 3 (Summer 1992*).

21 See Mats R. Berdal, "Whither UN Peacekeeping", *Adelphi Paper 281* (London: International Institute for Strategic Studies, 1993).

22 For an authoritative account, see Steven R. Ratner, *The New UN Peacekeeping* (New York: St. Martin's Press, 1995).

23 See UN Doc. A/55/305-S/2000/809. 21 August 2000, the report of the inquiry into peace-maintenance headed by Brahimi.

24 See Richard H. Ullman, ed., *The World and Yugoslavia's Wars* (New York: Council on Foreign Relations, 1996) and Woodward, *Balkan Tragedy.*

25 For an account from the Dutch perspective, that led to the resignation of the government, see Netherlands Institute for War Documentation, *Srebernica, a 'Safe' Area: Reconstruction, Background, Consequences, and Analysis of the Fall of a Safe Area* (Amsterdam: Boom Publishers, 2002).

26 See Jarat Chopra and Thomas G. Weiss, "Sovereignty is no longer sacrosanct: Codifying humanitarian intervention", *Ethics and International Affairs*, 6 (1992), 95–117; and International Commission on Intervention and State Sovereignty, *The Responsibility to Protect* (Ottawa: ICISS, 2001).

27 See Ratner, *The New UN Peacekeeping,* Chapter 7.

28 Edward Mortimer, "International Administration of War-Torn Societies, *Global Governance,* 10, 1 (2004), 13.

29 Alexandros Yannis, "The UN as government in Kosovo", *Global Governance,* 10, 1 (2004), 79.

30 See See UN Doc. A/55/305-S/2000/809. 21 August 2000, and the account of Annan's reorganization of the Secretariat, Chapter 3, above.
31 Hans Blix, the head of the inspection mission, gives his account in *Disarming Iraq: the Search for Weapons of Mass Destruction* (London: Bloomsbury, 2004).
32 Independant Inquiry Committe into the United Nations Oil-for-Food Programme, *Interim Report* (New York, 2005); available on www.iic-offp.org
33 For an unusual first-person observation of efficiency in the field, see Linda Polman, *We Did Nothing: why the truth doesn't always come out when the UN goes in* (London: Viking, 2003). See also Dallaire, *Shake Hands with the Devil,* and Michael N. Barnett, *Eyewitness to a Genocide: the United Nations and Rwanda* (Ithaca, NY: Cornell University Press, 2002).

5 Promoting global general welfare

1 See Preamble, UN Charter.
2 Article 1, 3 and Article 55.
3 My calculation from the table on p. 21, UN Doc. A/58/6 (Introduction), 16 April 2003, *Proposed Programme Budget for Biennium 2004–2005.* This calculation excludes the separate account for peacekeeping missions in the field that are financed by dedicated contributions from UN members.
4 For the governments nominating the members and the relevant ECOSOC resolutions, see UN doc. E/2203/L.1/Add.6, 26 March 2004.
5 Article 71. For insights into the vast realm of NGOs, see Thomas G. Weiss and Leon Gordenker (eds), *NGOS, the UN, and Global Governance* (Boulder, CO: Lynne Rienner, 1996).
6 For an extended treatment, see Schechter (ed.), *United Nations-Sponsored World Conferences.*
7 Fomerand, "UN Conferences: Media Events…", 361.
8 See Murphy, *International Organization…* ; and David Mitrany, *A Working Peace System* (Chicago: Quadrangle Books, 1966). Mitrany's book was first published in 1943.
9 See George Schild, *Bretton Woods and Dumbarton Oaks: American Economic and Political Postwar Planning in the Summer of 1994* (New York: St. Martin's Press, 1996) which tracks the beginnings of the international financial institutions.
10 Its legal foundation is ECOSOC Resolution 13 (III).
11 Louis Emmerij, Richard Jolly and Thomas G. Weiss, *Ahead of the Curve? UN Ideas and Global Challenges*, 73. This is the first volume of a series of studies of the intellectual history of the UN. For new publications in the UN Intellectual History Project, see Internet website www.unhistory.org.
12 This section and what follows relies heavily on Emmerij, *Ahead of the Curve,* especially chapters 2 and 3.
13 Emmerij, *Ahead of the Curve,* 29.
14 For a brief overview of this evolution, see Thomas G. Weiss, David P. Forsythe, and Roger A. Coate, *The United Nations and Changing World Poltiics,* 4th ed.(Boulder, CO: Westview, 2004), 221–41.
15 Emmerij, *Ahead of the Curve,* 55 ff.

16 See Yves Berthelot, ed., *Unity and Diversity in Development Ideas: Perspective from the UN Regional Commissions* (Bloomington, IN: Indiana University Press, 2004), for a fuller treatment of this little-explored realm.
17 Berthelot, *Unity and Diversity,* 49.
18 Initially organized without the Caribbean region which was added later.
19 Berthelot, *Unity and Diversity,* 181–91, traces the development and persuasiveness of Prebisch's work.
20 For an account of this development, see Robert L. Rothstein, *Global bargaining: UNCTAD and the Quest for a New International Economic Order* (Princeton, NJ: Princeton University Press, 1979).
21 For a profound analysis of this transformation, see Mathias Finger and Bérangère Magarinos-Ruchat, "The Transformation of International Public Organizations: The Case of UNCTAD," in Dijkzeul and Beigbeder, *Rethinking International Organizations,* 140–65.
22 For a brief overview, see Weiss, Forsythe and Coate, *The United Nations and Changing World Politics,* 267–71. The enormous documentation is reviewed in Shanna Halpern, *The United Nations Conference on Environment and Development: Process and Documentation* (Providence, RI, Academic Council on the United Nations System, 1992).
23 His reflections were published as Maurice Strong, *Where on Earth Are We Going?*, New York, Norton, 2001.
24 Lie, *In the Cause of Peace.*
25 See John P. Humphrey, *Human Rights and the United Nations: a Great Adventure* (Dobbs Ferry, NY, Transnational Publications, 1984) for a participant's account.
26 This lecture is reprinted with annotations in Adam Roberts and Benedict Kingsbury (eds.), *United Nations, Divided World: The UN's Roles in International Relations*, 2nd ed.(Oxford: Clarendon Press, 1993). The quotation is on 193.
27 Waldheim, *In the Eye of the Storm,* Chapter 9.
28 See UN Doc. GA/Res/57/313. The Secretary-General reported to the 2004 General Assembly on a series of reforms in UN Doc. A/58/569.
29 Weiss, Forsythe and Coate, *The United Nations and Changing World Politics,* 167.
30 Nobel Prize lecture, UN Press Release SG/SM/8071, Oct. 12, 2001.
31 UN Press Release SG/SM/8071.
32 UN Press Release SG/T.2405, April 8, 2004; "10 Years after Rwanda Genocide, Annan unveils plan to stop future massacres", UN News Centre, www.un.org.
33 See also the searching critique by Alex de Waal in Dijkzeul and Beigbeder, *Rethinking International Organizations*, Chapter 8.

6 Reaching out to broader publics

1 See his account in Lie, *In the Cause of Peace,* 249–70.
2 See detailed account in Urquhart, *Hammarskjöld,* 261–92. Urquhart also authoritatively treats the Hammarskjöld idea of preventive diplomacy here.
3 An outstanding example is the speech at Oxford University, 30 May 1961, "The International Civil Servant in Law and Fact", UN Press Release SG/1035.

4 See his account in Thant, *View From the UN,* 57–91.

5 For a detailed accounts, see Pérez de Cuéllar, *Pilgrimage for Peace.*

6 UN Doc. A/41/1, *Annual Report of the Secretary-General on the Work of the Organization* (1998), 1.

7 UN Doc. A/46/1, *Report of the Secretary-General on the Work of the Organization* (1991), 1

8 Boutros-Ghali, *The Unvanquished* ... , 26.

9 UN Doc. A/47/277/S-24111, 17 June 1992.

10 UN Doc. A/48/935, 6 May 1994.

11 See his account in *The Unvanquished,* 251–56.

12 See "Report of the Secretary-General on the Work of the Organization", UN Doc. A/54/1 (1977), 3.

13 For a complete account, Jacques Fomerand with Brendan Monahan, "The UN Secretary-General as an Actor in International Politics: the Need for Leadership", in The Japan Association for United Nations Studies, *The United Nations as a Global Actor* (Tokyo: Japan Association for United Nations Studies), 87–113.

14 "We the peoples of the United Nations", UN doc. A/54/2000, 13 April 2000.

15 "We the peoples ... ", 8.

16 My calculations based on UN Doc. A/58/6, "Proposed programme budget for the biennium 2004–2005", Introduction. Appropriations vary somewhat from year to year but generally have held around these magnitudes, 21.

17 UN General Assembly Res. 58/126, 19 December 2003.

18 The elements of the unceasing debate were set out more than 45 years ago in Leon Gordenker, "Policy-Making and Secretariat Influence in the UN General Assembly: The Case of Public Information", *American Political Science Review*, LIV, 2 (June 1960).

19 UN General Assembly Res. 13 I.

20 Statement by Shashi Tharoor, interim head of DPI, at Committee on Information, 22 April 2002. He refers to "We the Peoples".

21 UN Doc. A/AC.198/2003/2, a report by the Secretary-General to the Committee on Information, titled "Reorientation of United Nations activities in the field of public information and communications".

22 UN doc. A/AC.198/2004/6, "Better publicizing the work and decisions of the General Assembly", 23 February 2004.

23 Gordenker, "What U.N. Principles?: U.S. Debate on Iraq", *Global Governance,* 9,3 (July–Sept. 2003).

24 For significance of survey data, see Luck, *Mixed Messages,* 268–79.

7 Conclusion

1 Dag Hammarskjöld, *Markings* (New York: Alfred A. Knopf Co., 1944). This is a translation from the original Swedish.

Select bibliography

Boutros-Ghali, Boutros (1999) *Unvanquished: A US–UN Saga,* New York: Random House. Virulent, witty polemic strewn with details of his defeat for a second term as Secretary-General, it also illustrates the diplomatic role of a declared activist.

Dallaire, Roméo (2003) *Shake Hands With the Devil : The Failure of Humanity in Rwanda,* Toronto: Random House Canada.

Dijkzeul, Dennis and Beigbeder, Yves (eds) (2003) *Rethinking International Organizations: Pathology and Promise,* New York: Berghahn Books. Expert, unusual essays with the accent on management both of policy processes and execution. Annotated, no bibliography.

Gordenker, Leon, Coate, Roger A., Jonsson, Christer and Soderholm, Peter (1995) *International Cooperation in Response to Aid,* London: Pinter. Treats the way in which transnational networks contributed to placing the AIDS issue on the international agenda.

Goulding, Marrack (2002) *Peacemonger,* London: John Murray. A rare literate, frank view of working at the top of the Secretariat.

Lie, Trygve (1954) *In the Cause of Peace: Seven Years with the United Nations,* New York: Macmillan. Recollections by the first Secretary-General who willy-nilly laid down some lasting organizational foundations.

Luck, Edward C. (1999) *Mixed Messages: American Politics and International Organization 1919–1999,* Washington: Brookings Institution Press. A lively, balanced treatment by a veteran observer of crucial topics in the US–UN relationship with special attention to Washington politics. Annotated, no bibliography.

Murphy, Craig N. (1994) *International Organization and Industrial Change: Global Governance since 1850,* New York: Oxford University Press. An informed analysis of the growth of transnational organization, based on Gramsci's theories. Extensive bibliography.

Nassif, Ramses (1988) *U Thant in New York, 1961–71: A Portrait of the Third UN Secretary-General,* London: C. Hurst. More a snapshot than a painting, this memoir by Thant's press officer contains classified documents that give the flavor of the Secretary-General at work on high politics, especially the Cuban missile crisis and Viet Nam.

Newman, Edward (1998) *The UN Secretary-General from the Cold War to the New Era: A Global Peace and Security Mandate,* New York: St Martin's Press. A careful, scholarly account of the Secretary-General as a political operative with special attention to Péréz de Cuéllar and Boutros-Ghali. Annotated, no bibliography.

Pérez de Cuéllar, Javier (1997) *Pilgrimage for Peace: A Secretary-General's Memoir,* New York: St Martin's Press. Concentrates almost exclusively on security issues; it gives an inside, if pedestrian, account of his preoccupation with peace in Central America.

Rivlin, Benjamin and Gordenker, Leon (eds) (1993) *The Challenging Role of the UN Secretary-General,* Westport, CT: Praeger. Informed essays written at a moment of promise for an activist Secretary-General. Extensive bibliography.

Ruggie, John Gerard (1996) *Winning the Peace: America and World Order in the New Era*, New York: Columbia University Press. A keen, succinct analysis with extensive documentation.

Shevchekno, Arkady N. (1985) *Breaking with Moscow,* New York: Knopf. Moscow's man in Secretariat top defects.

Thant, U. (1977) *U Thant: View from the UN,* Newton Abbot, Devon: David and Charles. Incidents and a few strong side comments on crises and political issues by Hammarskjöld's reluctant successor who refers to his Buddhist beliefs but hardly touches either on the Secretariat or its individual members. Some unusual documents. No bibliography.

United Nations internet page: http://www.un.org. Maintained by the UN Department of Public Information, this site offers free access to most published UN documentation, both connected with deliberation in UN organs and general information. The internet page includes links to the services offered correspondents and to other organizations in the UN system.

Urquhart, Brian (1972) *Hammarskjöld,* New York: Harper and Row. A brilliant biography of the second Secretary-General by a close, keen associate. Annotated; no bibliography.

Waldheim, Kurt (1986) *In the Eye of the Storm: A Memoir,* Bethesda, MD: Adler and Adler. Events and episodes in 10 years as Secretary-General, it is evasive about his past as a Wehrmacht officer in WWII. It contains a chapter on managing the Secretariat. No bibliography.

Weiss, Thomas G (ed.) (1998) *Beyond UN Subcontracting,* Houndsmill, Basingstoke: Macmillan. Essays treating devolution of UN tasks in the field of security. The UN Secretariat figures in most of the treated cases. Bibliography.

Weiss, Thomas G. and Gordenker, Leon (eds) (1996) *NGOs, the UN and Global Governance,* Boulder, CO: Lynne Rienner. Analytical, informed treatments of the role of NGOs in important global issues. The UN Secretariat figures in most of these cases. Bibliography.

Index